Weird Girl
Adventures

From A to Z

SHELLEY BROWN
Weird Girl Adventures

FOREWORD BY

KIMBERLY DAVIS
Author, *Brave Leadership*

Weird Girl Adventures from A to Z – 1st ed.
Shelley Brown
www.WeirdGirlAdventures.com

Cover Design by AlyBlue Media, LLC
Interior Design by AlyBlue Media LLC
Published by AlyBlue Media, LLC

ISBN: 978-1-950712-42-7
AlyBlue Media, LLC
Ferndale, WA 98248
www.AlyBlueMedia.com

PRINTED IN THE UNITED STATES OF AMERICA

Testimonials

"The first time I heard Shelley speak it took about two seconds before I realized how beautifully bizarre she was. Then I read this book and it confirmed everything twice over. I would write whatever Shelley asked me to but after reading this, I will NEVER get a massage with her." —CHRIS TREW, author *How to Build a Comedy Scene from Scratch*

"Shelley Brown is all about authenticity. Come as you are. Be as you are. Accept who you are. *Weird Girl Adventures* is filled with stories that will have you laughing so hard you're GOING to pee, crying because you feel all the FEELS, nodding because HELL YEAH you think the same thing, gasping because it's just so wild it can't possibly be TRUE and yet it is true, and BECOMING empowered to lean just a little bit further into your weird." —TERESA QUINLAN, founder of IQ+ EQ+TQ

"If you ever thought you might be weird and it has left you doubting yourself, hiding who you are, or feeling disconnected from others, you are not alone. Most of us grow up thinking we have to be like others to fit in, to belong, when really we have to be ourselves to feel at home in the company of others. Shelley Brown shines a fresh light on the judgment we might have been left with after experiences that didn't quite fit what we expected, and shows us how to cherish ourselves with all the quirks that make us beautiful humans." —JEANETTE BRONÉE, Rethinker, culture strategist, author and speaker.

"A collection of short essays full of inspiration, reality, and humor, Shelley Brown's book will bring sensations of nostalgia and relief. Nostalgia for the aspects of childhood you remember as good and hopeful, and relief to be in a place where you know you can choose to move forward, to be different from who you were as a child and young adult, to be mindful of where you are now and comfortable with your past. I could read these all day, over and over again."
—SARAH ELKINS, chief storymaker, Elkins Consulting Inc

"Calling all the weird ones! Proof positive that you're not alone. Shelley Brown's compilation of sweet, salty and deliciously snack-sized tales will make you laugh, cry, nod, and most of all celebrate your own weirdness." —LESLIE EHM, WSJ, USA Today and Amazon #1 bestselling author of *Swagger*

"Shelley brings to light the fact that our differences and our weird is truly what connects us. She opens up her wonderful world of weird to us in short snippets of her beautiful and complex life. We all feel shame, regret, joy, elation, and dis-appointment. Shelley affirms that in these margins we truly can celebrate our humanity. As an ER physician, I've seen so many mental health crises. Framing our mind-set the way Shelley does, through celebrating and allowing our weird, is a step in the right direction to healing our souls." —ERICA LOCKE, MD, FAAEM, FAAFP

Shelley Brown's *Weird Girl Adventures* is quirky, witty, charming and the perfect fit for any woman who's ever felt out of place in her own skin. Weird Girl Adventures is the chicken soup we all need right now. —LINDSAY SUTHERLAND BOAL, founder, SHE WALKS, women's life & purpose coach

"A refreshingly quirky collection of stories that hold a mirror up for us to recall the weird moments of our own lives, reminding us that the strange little tidbits of things remembered are to be embraced as they shaped us—for better or worse—yet we decide what defines us. Brilliant!" —JULIE SCOTT, self expansion coach, speaker, author

"Ready for a big ole slice of humble pie ala mode? Served up with a side of hilarity and nostalgia and a whole bunch of I-can-relate? Then you're in the right club. Shelley Brown pulls the curtain back for those of us who never quite fit in, who are a special kind of weird, those of us who have spent a lifetime ready for a book like this—a book of tales to celebrate the weirdness that dwells in us all. Liberating! Powerful!"
—JENNI JO, Tension Tamer®, Massage Therapist to the Rockstars

"If you've ever felt that you were alone in your *not-fitting-in*-ness, your *why does this only happen to me*-ness, or your . . . weirdness, then Shelley Brown wrote this delightful book just for you. This vignette-filled tour of her charming, tragic, alarming, and often laugh-out-loud world, she shows us all how being weird—and loving what that looks like for you—is the key to living a full and altogether human life."
—TAMSEN WEBSTER, founder and chief message strategist, Find the Red Thread

"Shelley Brown captures the essence of what it means to be human with her beautiful, poignant, funny, and lyrical voice. We all have that thing that makes us unique and different, yet we all want to fit in and be like others. What makes us truly connect with others is allowing ourselves to be who we are, allowing others to be their true selves. This is what Shelley calls 'our weird.' I'll take it!" —KATE MACKINNON, Feng Shui expert, speaker, TedX 2020, mentor

"To be human is to embrace our imperfection. This book so beautifully invites people to understand that our uniqueness is our competitive advantage." —BRYAN KRAMER, author of Human-to-Human, TED speaker

"Equal parts honest, raw, funny, and empowering, *Weird Girl Adventures* is a call to action for those who are caught in betwixt and in between who they are and who the world expect them to be. If you are struggling to live your truth, let Shelley Brown ignite your path."
—LAURA GASSNER OTTING, WashPost bestselling author of *Limitless*

Dedication

This book is dedicated to all of you weird people, those I know and those I've yet to know, and to those I love—my little family, River and Mark Brown (no relation) who provide me with the greatest gift of all— laughter on a daily basis.

This book is also dedicated to the woman who is etched on my heart, my false-eyelashed, feminist and fascinating force of a mom whose legacy will only and forever be referred to by both first and last name.

Finally, I dedicate this book to my late father, Gerald Brown. You were the funniest man I knew, and wish with my entire being that you were here to share this with me. I miss you beyond words.

Contents

BY KIMBERLY DAVIS

Foreword

I think I've spent my life looking for my own reflection. I don't think I'm special that way, I think most of us do the same. We look for ourselves in the shows we watch, in the memes we share, and in the strangers we pass in the grocery store or in Starbucks, or when walking our dogs in the park (not that I have a dog, but if I did, I would). We long for evidence that, with all our quirks and foibles, we're okay.

That is the great gift of this book.

When most of what we consume is airbrushed, anesthetized, and sculpted to perfection, Shelley Brown dares to share raw, real, and inescapably human weird girl adventures. In doing so, she gives us a chance to look at our own strange selves with more compassionate eyes.

You know how when you laugh so hard that you start to get the hiccups, or feel like you have to go to the bathroom, or pray that your hiccups don't cause you to go to the bathroom sooner than you can get there? Well, that was my experience in reading this book. If Erma Bombeck, Glennon Doyle and Lucille Ball all stirred their DNA into what would become one giant gluten-free cake, Shelley Brown will pop out of that cake sporting pink cropped hair and a tiara.

Shelley and I both share the distinct privilege of having grown up in the 1980s, which makes this book a particularly trippy joyride for me, yet you don't need to have lived through The Breakfast Club and Madonna to appreciate the absurdity of your own adolescence. Shelley takes us all back in her shag carpeted time machine to revisit the insecure days of our youth. She invites us to play Barbies, hang out with her behind the bleachers, and share a meal near the airplane bathroom.

Readers revisit all those what-was-I-thinking moments in life, and cull out the lessons learned and then thank God for how far you've come. You get to laugh so hard you cry and then, when you least expect it, find yourself gasping for air because you've just been hit in the solar plexus by a truth so powerful that it takes your breath away.

For more than a decade, I've been doing work around authenticity and bravery. I've had thousands of conversations with people about why brave matters. It turns out that the one unifying characteristic of everyone who risks showing up as their most authentic self is bravery.

Shelley Brown is both laugh-out-loud funny and achingly authentic. She lowers the protective mask that most of us wear in our daily lives, and plays the soundtrack of her innermost thoughts, to give us all the greatest gift there is—permission to be human. Weirdly, wonderfully human.

I believe our brave unfolds one situation at a time. Allow Shelley's authenticity to summon your authenticity.

Let her brave ignite yours. One. Chapter. At. A. Time.

KIMBERLY DAVIS
Founder & Author, *Brave Leadership*
Braveleadershipbook.com
Onstageleadership.com

BY SHELLEY BROWN

Preface

Life is like a very long Afterschool Special. Some of you may remember them, and if you are too young, just envision a pre-Netflix series about the average controversial, dramatic, traumatizing, complicated life situation followed by a solution except the solution isn't a half-hour episode, it's a journey and a continuum. It's this weird life!

Sometimes our weird doesn't know it's weird until our weirding is judged by others in an indelible way. For example, at a precarious, prepubescent pimply period in my life, otherwise known as age twelve, my journal was discovered by my classmates, the very journal in which I had scrawled pictures of female peers with one arrow indicating those who had developed boobs and another arrow had a Y or N pointing to their va-jay-jay to indicate those who had started her period. The discovery of my private journal led to relentless bullying along with my first suicide attempt with three aspirin.

The moral of my story is that at times it feels as though our weird is growing while at the same time we're trapped in a downward elevator with no buttons. Our inner weird person thinks each floor is the bottom, yet the elevator continues to go downward.

The weird elevator opens into my middle-class suburban home where my fascinating, fear-inspiring mom is at the forefront of the dig-your-heels-in-and-get-out-of-my-way feminist movement, striving to obtain some modicum of recognition and success while simultaneously succumbing to societal pressures to be thin, beautiful, and forever youthful.

My dad is a hippie Mensa veterinarian born ten years too early. He is the funniest man in the world when not suffering from his own rage and perfectionism, which he projects onto everyone.

And my sister, when we are not in the same room fighting, is in her room with the door locked plotting her escape.

I grew up confused. Everyone was so isolated in their own messed-up bubble of struggle. You know, the struggles we all have in life that cause chaos, fighting, yelling, breaking things, depression, stress, and dysfunction. Somehow this translates into a huge space of isolation and loneliness, later defined as the proverbial I-am-not-enough that plagues so many of us.

I escaped the chaos, confusion, and uncertainty in all the pink things in my pink bedroom where possibility over-shadowed problems—until it doesn't.

And then that thing happened with my journal . . .

The elevator doors close. This thing is going down.

"Lower level one," says the elevator lady, though this elevator had no lady, just a voice, maybe from hell. This low level of self-hatred offered me a new high school. It also featured drugs, boys, diets and cigarettes. I loved cigarettes. They made dieting easier, and no one bullied me there.

"Lower level two," said the elevator lady. Promiscuity, bulimia, anorexia, and daddy issues. Hmm, sounds lonely and horrible. I think I'll get off on this floor for a few years. Oops, who am I kidding—a few decades. I explored around and found therapists and treatment centers to try on for a zillion dollars. Okay, that was nice and slightly unhelpful. I didn't know I'd have to sleep with all those guys, try to make my daddy love me, and clean up so much vomit.

"Lower level three," the lady announced. Late eighties, early nineties. I really can't remember much other than affairs, cheating, a broken compass, more vomit, and an angry mom who I apparently, "NEVER LISTEN TO."

"Lower level four." Love and marriage, miscarriage, marathons and motorcycles.

"Lower level five." If it looks good, it is no good. This was my real-life Instagram before Instagram. A world before selfie rings where you actually had to look like the real deal in the real world while your inner world is crumbling.

"Lower level six." Crack, back, shiver, shake and shatter. This is where I feared the elevator would stop forever. The doors opened to a roomful of people smoking crack, including the ghost of my Prince Charming, the once beautiful man who was sure to rescue me. In disbelief, I entered on a newly fused spine and wobbly legs, minus a couple other body parts, and shaking with anxiety. Here, the pieces of my life rolled away like marbles scattering into unreachable spaces. This is a living nightmare. Where is the call button? I need to leave *now*.

"Lower level seven." Welcome to fight-or-flight, the gift from a lifetime of anxiety topped by the unimaginable experiences of floor six. Here, I found one nervous breakdown after another, all for the cost of a bunch of new jobs due to job probation or getting fired, and failed attempts to make everything in life work while I went from zero to catastrophe in seconds until I finally fell into even smaller pieces.

Weird Girl Adventures is a compilation of my own weird experiences that go from the bottom level to the top floor of impossibility—you don't have to like it, love it, or embrace it. Simply allow. This is my invitation to you. When we allow our weird, who knows what else is possible? The journey in between is where Weird Girl Adventures come in.

I wrote this book for all of us weird girls because the circle of Kumbaya continues to should-shame us into believing that simply by listening to or following them, somehow we'll begin to magically love ourselves just because they tell us we should. I call bull-should.

The strongest feelings we sense in isolation also happen to be the things that connects us most—our weird, or, as I like to say, our collective humanness of weirding. It's the same weirdness I felt when not knowing the right answer to the proverbial chicken question. No, no not that one. It was when my germaphobe mother asked if I rinsed my chicken before I cooked it, and I had to really hedge my bets on how to respond. I answered wrong and will never forget her words, "Don't rinse your chicken!"

These words are forever etched onto my weirdness and sprinkled over so many of these stories. This book is a roller-coaster to a freight train down a rabbit hole, but isn't life?

Sometimes the ride is long, sometimes it's short, but the train is always moving and we can get off any time we want.

This book is also grounded in joy, the same joy I had playing with Barbies in my pink-filled bedroom, with pink-filled dreams where I sat clothed in possibility. It's a journey through the extraordinary of the ordinary where thoughts so many of us have yet never say out loud get to dance, play, cry, lament and mostly weird in this achingly beautiful thing we call life.

If you recognize yourself in this book, thank you. If you laugh along with me, at me and at yourself, thank you. If you recognize this life is really the same dog different paws, thank you. If you embrace the collective usness of us . . . thank you.

The Glue is Drying is a poem I wrote about pieces of myself falling off, and pieces I give away. I'd pick up these pieces and began to hold onto the ones I chose to keep through allowing my own weirdness.

The glue begins to dry when we choose to let go of the suffering and realize we can continually pick up the pieces as well as let go of the pieces that no longer serve us. The glue doesn't dry until we die.

> Shattered shards, broken glass
> Kicked in heart, fell on ass
> Pieces of myself I once knew cracked and broken
> Held by glue . . .

Done dying, the glue is drying.

SHELLEY BROWN | Weird Girl Adventures
www.WeirdGirlAdventures.com
shelley@weirdgirladventures.com

CHAPTER 1

Are you there, God? It's me, Shelley

Are you there, God?

It's me, Shelley.

Remember how excited we were about that special thing that happens around age twelve? Judy Blume is now eighty-something and you'd think she would've have given enough of a crap to write the sequel.

I'm a weird girl, and aging is weird. I'm not unhappy about it, it's just weird and weird stuff happens. I won't bore you with any of the details or include before and after pictures, but I am here to tell you there is a conspiracy theory.

The theory is that women have a secret pact about not telling younger women the shit that's gonna happen as they age. I naturally blame Judy for this.

So there is a saying,

> "If you want to know what a woman is
> going to look like when she gets
> older, look at her mother."

I think my weird mother is beautiful and I don't mind you looking at her as a benchmark as long as she is sitting down. If you want to date me, you may think, "Hmmm, she's attractive. I wonder what her mother looks like?"

I am really sad that my weird mom lives in California, but on the other hand, if she lived here and you met her, you may think, "Hmmm. Her weird mom is attractive for her age. Shelley may age pretty well," but then. *But then,* my mom would stand up and she's like four-foot-eight and you may be like, "Game over."

My weird mom won't even tell the doctor how tall she is. She tells him what she wants her height to be and says in earnest, "You'll just have trust me."

By the way, Mr. I'm So Tall, you too are going to shrink and someday you may have to stand on your tiptoes and raise your hand when you are standing at the deli case like I do in order to be helped.

Are you there, God? It's me, Shelley.

CHAPTER 2

Agony and ecstasy

I came back in 2013, thinking, "I am no longer who I think you thought I was."

You didn't care. You embraced me and gave me a warm, most gracious welcome.

I left you in 2010 to fulfill my desire to live out who I thought I was, and who I thought you thought I was. I told you I was leaving to run distance year-round in a warmer climate. Maybe I didn't tell you the other reasons, including a geographical cure from a string of general fuckups, bad romances, train-wrecked friendships and my inability to emancipate myself from my totally enmeshed relationship with my mom.

Oh, and also perhaps to straighten out the arrow on my moral compass.

You gave me a beautiful sendoff, and so warmly and graciously wished me well to go be the person I thought you thought I was and who I thought I was.

Moving to North Carolina, I had a ball, then sat on a wall, had a great fall and went tumbling down a rabbit hole of darkness, smoke and mirrors.

I couldn't run my way out of this one, so I started writing frantically to purge the fear, anger and the deep depths of grief from losing who I thought I was, who I thought you thought I was, who I thought someone else was, and who I thought I was to him but wasn't. My friends in North Carolina performed emotional triage and sent me on my way. Warmly and graciously, they wished me well to go be the person I was made to be.

So here we are again.

You loved me, encouraged me, and supported all my endeavors. You provided me with depth, breath and levity, fueling my creativity, fueling my truth and passions. You fed my emotional wellness with love and kindness.

After five years, I'm leaving again. Thank you for so graciously and warmly wishing me well to continue being who I am. May you be happy, may you be healthy. May you be safe, may you live with ease.

CHAPTER 3

Barney's dead

"Can you come over and make my hair purple?" I texted the guy who does my color.

He texted me back, "Sure."

He came over Friday afternoon and applied purple dye to my hair. Now, I am not afraid of color. My hair has been pink, purple and blue this year alone. I thought since I didn't have to travel until mid-September, I could have a little fun with my hair color. Well . . . it turned into a purple nightmare.

Holy Purple Rain! It looked like I had killed Barney, and his purple DNA was splattered over both me and the bathroom. I won't go into great detail about what happened, but suffice it to say that my hair guy told me to wash my hair in thirty minutes and then left.

I looked in the bathroom mirror. This looks awfully dark, like Grape Ape dark, I thought. I got into the shower, closed my eyes, rinsed my hair, opened my eyes, and saw nothing but purple.

SOS! I have fallen into a bottle
of Welch's grape juice.

The entire shower was purple, my hands were purple, and my body was purple. Holy eggplant! This was insane.

I dried off my hair, turning the towel purple. I looked in the mirror and my face was purple. It's as if I am in the movie *Carrie* but the blood was violet, like a Smerf of a different ethnicity. Holy grape Nehi!

Now I'm worried about my skin but more concerned that I am going to have to replace the entire bathroom. How am I going to tell my friends I have to cancel plans because I am purple?

I had no idea what to do. I took Tide laundry detergent into the shower and washed my hair. The purple floodgates reopen. I then filled the sink with hot water and Tide and began rubbing my face vigorously with a washcloth. It's working! I scrubbed and scrubbed and my skin slowly went from cabbage to violet and then faded.

I used bleach to clean the bathroom and just know that if the forensic investigators came and sprayed that murder scene stuff, the entire bathroom would reveal all of the Barney's DNA. Thank God the bleach worked and I didn't have to pay for a whole new bathroom.

Any plum pudding, I went out with my friends that night and we had a great time even though my hair looked like Smucker's grape jelly.

The next morning I woke in a purple haze and my white pillowcase was now purple. I went to the bathroom to look at my hair. Ugh. I grabbed Dawn dishwashing liquid and washed my hair three times. My body is again purple and I have to wash with Tide once more.

That's it, Alice Walker didn't write about this and Oprah isn't here to star in this movie. I am done. I called my friend who cuts my hair to ask if she can help. She said yes. Potato, my dog and I walked over to salon. Several hours later, we lost the war on color correction.

My dear friends did everything they could, but it was a lost cause. I was tired, Potato was tired and my hair was tired, broken, damaged and now an indescribable shade of yellow.

I walked down the street with my yellow head crying the entire way home. I got home, put on a hat, and cried more.

My girlfriend came over. When I took off my hat, a slight gasp escaped her mouth. That's it, I'm going to shave my head, I thought. And that's exactly what I did. The minute I made this decision, I felt relief. I had no idea how it was going to turn out, but I didn't care.

This was another valuable reminder that sometimes the shit that I think is important, the crap that I let get to me doesn't mean a thing. I am fortunate in that even though there was no saving my hair, some people have to do this for more devastating reasons.

It is just hair and nothing more. It's not my health, my friends or my family. I am constantly learning my identity isn't in what I do, the relationship I am in, the job I have or what I look like. My identity is just who I am.

As my hair fell to the floor, so did all
the stuff that was bothering me.

It just doesn't matter.

Love,

Shelley

CHAPTER 4

Catholic

Holy homily! Jesus, Mary and Joseph! Catholic! Yes, I wanted to be Catholic! As a little girl, my aspirations were to become Barbie, a playboy bunny, or a stewardess, all Catholics.

I had a strong desire to be a Catholic. Not because of the skirts, knee-socks, saints or even because of Jesus himself, but because I thought anyone who wasn't Jewish was Catholic, and that meant their lives were perfect. Somehow I knew Tabitha, Marcia, and every other person I sat too close to the TV watching, was a Catholic.

I knew the secret that Catholics were happier. They had happy homes, did happy things and always smiled. Those Catholics were the ones with vans that had shag carpeting, a mini kitchen and an exterior acrylic lacquer detailing a magnificent stallion born of a fiery orange-yellow sunrise.

Without a doubt, Barbie was a Catholic. There is no way a Jewish girl could look like that.

Any apostle, the only frame of reference I had for nuns was the flying one who seemed very sweet and benign. I had never met a priest but I figured since everyone referred to them as Father, they had to be kind. Those Catholics seemed brighter and shinier, especially when leaving church, well, on TV anyway.

Catholics threw rice and stuff while us Jews went to dark, somber temples speaking in some phlegmy language I didn't understand. Yes, I wanted to be one of those Catholics.

Catholics had more holidays involving candy. Being the biggest candy junkie on the planet, I was consumed with jealousy, dejected and wistful looking at those remarkable Easter baskets filled with every sort of cavity-inducing sugary delight. If that wasn't enough to deflate my Hamantoshin heart, the basket had a stuffed animal, too! Holy hot cross buns, the unfairness! The anguish! The lack of colored eggs!

Catholic kids played games like communion, confession and confirmation while I was relegated to hide in my friend's musty, dark crawlspace always delegated to playing the role of Anne Frank while she played the role of the Nazi prison guard giving me bread crust and one sip of water.

Do you want to come over and play Sit Shiva? Holy Hadassah! Good times.

Those Catholics had better families, too, usually involveing more than the average two children homes of most Jews. Large families, yes! I loved the Catholics with the large families, the commotion, activities, lots of shoes, and moms in aprons cooking family dinners. Catholic grandmothers with ample bosom were always smiling and giving me homemade cake. The Catholics had more barbeques, too! Oh, and Christmas, need I say more? Oh wait, yes I do, matching plaid clothing items.

I did end up marrying a Catholic
who ate ham sandwiches
on white bread.

I, on the other hand, had ham shame. At the deli counter, in my usual low and loud voice, I would order sliced turkey loud and proud, but then turn meek, quiet and look both ways before whispering my ham order. I am not so sure it was about the ham. It could be the fact that it was Krakus Ham. It was hard for me to order "crack-ass ham."

Any Archbishop, I later learned that not everyone who wasn't Jewish was not a Catholic, but must admit that a little bit of my childhood perception still lingers and I still believe Barbie is a shiksa for shiz. I know there is no shame in ham, not all nuns are kind, and no family is perfect.

I could go on and on...Catholics wouldn't, but a Jew would.

Any pew, I'm a Jew.

From Catholic to Buddha.

Blessings to you.

May the Lord give you candy.

CHAPTER 5

Cats WTF

I wasn't going to make the first move. He stood there sizing me up, eyes unblinking, penetrating into the very core of my being. I stayed as still as I possibly could. I tried to be relaxed, gazing right past his shoulder. This went on for quite a few minutes until he turned and just walked away. I mean just like that, indifferent as if none of it really mattered. Cats! WTF?

Any apathy, I don't get cats at all. They either seem to look at me with indifference or as if they want to imbed their little sharp daggery nails into my eyeballs if they could, then walk away with indifference as if none of it really mattered. Cats! WTF?

Fluffy, Tiger, Shadow? Do they actually come when you call them, or only when they are feline like it?

I am trying to like cats, especially now that I am cat-sitting. I think my problem is that I want them to be like dogs, but they can't be like dogs because they are cats. It's like the old saying, "You can't get bread from the hardware store." Cats! WTF?

I don't get the term "scaredy cat." I do get scared of cats. I don't think cats are scared; I think they just run away because they don't want to be bothered. Maybe some cats are touch averse, but I don't think they are afraid. If they were so scared, they wouldn't return dead things to you. Cats! WTF?

I want to love cats because it's the cool thing to do now. No, really, I do want to love cats because they really are cute and because I cat-sit and don't want to be afraid they will scratch out my eyeballs. I don't particularly like pets that poop in the house, and have you taken a good whiff of a can cat food lately? Cats! WTF?

I recently accepted a cat-sitting job in my building. Like many cat lovers, the owner stated, "My cat is just like a dog," as she successfully held her cat in her lap for twenty seconds before it jumped out to look out the window at nothing.

Your cat is not like a dog.
Cats! WTF?

My father was the city cat doctor. Yes, a feline-only veterinarian for his last fifteen years. We never had cats in our home and when asked if he had cats, my father could have referred to the vet clinic blood-donor cat, but what he really wanted to say and what he told me was,

"You don't have to have a pussy
to be a gynecologist."

Dad! WTF?

The bottom line is you don't have to understand something to like it, and you don't have to understand someone to like them. Me! WTF? Cat people, don't get mad at me-ow.

CHAPTER 6

Cleaning my closet

I realized that like so many people, I had too many clothes in my closet. Some people keep clothes because they will *someday* lose enough weight to fit into them. Some keep clothes because they were really expensive, and some people keep clothes for nostalgic reasons.

I have come to realize that in my life I have spent many years wearing clothes that are ill-fitting, buying clothes and returning them, wearing things that were unflattering, things that weren't made well, things others bought for me, things others picked out for me, shoes that hurt my feet, coats that weren't warm enough....

Growing up I was dressed in the cutest little colorful matching shorts and tops, they were made of a fabric called Perfection, with one stripe the color of "Be a good girl so no one gets angry" and the other stripe the color of "If you say, jump, I have to ask how high?"

In elementary school I wore denim bellbottoms made of "I am not smart enough," and corky little platform shoes made of "How you look is the only thing that matters."

Throughout the years I wore tight-fitting jeans from designers named "Unpopular," and "You're not pretty enough," jumpsuits from "You're only good for a fuck," hats from "You are not allowed to say no," different pairs of socks made from "Unlovable," "Unworthy," and "Stupid."

I went through a phase of going to stores to try on clothes made from scratchy fibers including "Promiscuity" and "Eating disorder." Some of them were flattering for a short time but often cumbersome, bulky, and very, very costly.

I wore running shoes embellished with "Accomplishment," soles from "Accolades," laces made from "Look at me," medals made from "No pain, no gain."

For a while I wore dresses made from "Self-pity," "Poor me," and "Life sucks," but gave them up for the most expensive, beautiful gowns I've ever owned. One gown was luxurious and stunning, made from this exquisite fabric called "Love," embellished with pearls of "Promises" and lace in a pattern of "Lies and addiction." I loved this gown and wore it every day. When the stitching started to come undone, I mended it. When it got dirty, I cleaned it. I kept putting it back on but it got so stained, filthy, torn and tattered until I could no longer repair it. I stood there screaming, crying, broken, anxious, and fearful.

I cleaned out my closet and threw out the clothes that did not fit, the clothes that were old, the clothes that were stained, the clothes that were tight and the clothes that were loose until there was nothing in my closet.

I stand here naked, and see who I really am.

"If you get a pig, you can stop referring to yourself as one"

CHAPTER 7

Couples massage

Couple's massage? Why? I just don't get it. You're lying there naked, typically with eyes closed, while someone is rubbing ninety-plus percent of your naked body. What is the purpose of doing this in the same room as your significant other?

I remember my first couple's massage. It was about seven years ago. My boyfriend at the time said as we were disrobing, "Shelley, try not to talk during the massage."

Holy let go of an untied blown-up balloon ready to fart its exhale across the room! It was torture. I was practically biting my lip. I want to know about the person who is touching me in my birthday suit. Is that so wrong?

I want to know if they like their job, where they live, how long they've been a masseuse, and the worst thing that ever happened while massaging someone. Do they think couple's massages are stupid? I mean they can't even talk to the other masseuse massaging the other naked person.

Any un-ironic, last weekend, my boyfriend booked us a couple's massage. We used to go to Dancing Fingers when we lived in Chicago. While the name makes it sound a bit sketchy, it was relatively good, cheap and the added benefit was I had the ability to be unusually quiet because the massage therapists spoke only a few words of English.

There was one caveat though—we had to decide who would get Wendy and who would get the guy. I am pretty confident the guy had GERD, acid reflux or some type of GI problem. During the massage he would constantly clear his throat, and I could hear the gurgling of stomach acids some-where between his esophagus and throat. I would usually acquiesce and let boyfriend have Wendy, even though she accidently touched him in the non-ninetieth percentile area.

Wendy, "Ohhhh, sorry!"

Boyfriend, "It's okay."

We don't know Baltimore very well, however we are both very practical about money and will shop for a deal for a ridiculously inordinate amount of time. If time is money, we are definitely losers, if that makes cents.

So my boyfriend gets a deal on Groupon for a couple's massage. We get in the car and drive a few miles down streets that when you see the light changing to red, you think to yourself, *oh, shit.*

Many of the homes are boarded up and folks are pretty much hanging around the corner store looking a bit, shall we say, unwell from such things as, I'm guessing here, crack and liquor.

We finally get to the address, and I'm thinking this isn't such a great idea but we decide to brave it. We walk up to the door and are greeted by a little boy about nine years-old who ushers us into to a little room and tells us to wait while his mom is finishing up with another appointment.

He also instructs us to fill out some forms for the massage. We both take a pen with a fake flower attached by a stick by what look to be medical adhesive tape. We are both on the same page as neither of us write down our true personal information.

The little room is filled with decorative items one would find at a place such as Home Goods, including little canvases and boxes fashioned with positive messages of love and kindness. These items are offset by the mismatched drapes, broken chairs and curtain panel serving as a tablecloth on a makeshift desk that holds a fax machine. There is no air conditioning and it's close to ninety degrees outside, but there is a fan, so we sit there. Mark is in the broken armchair and every so often he peeks out the window to see if the car is still there.

"MELISSAAAAAAAAA! MELISSAAAA!" Some woman is yelling at the door.

I yell back, "She's with a client."

Another boy about twelve goes to the door and I decide to follow him. The woman asks the kid, "Whose car is that? It's a five-hundred-dollar fine. That's a handicap zone."

Boyfriend moves the car because we don't want to lose five hundred dollars in the process of walking away from the one-hundred-twenty dollars we prepaid for the massage.

We try to stay patient but begin to think this is all a scam. Maybe the trick is that folks who pay for the Groupon can no longer wait it out and just leave.

Boyfriend decides to text the masseuse to inform her we're sitting in her waiting room. While he is doing this, I notice her cellphone charging next to the fax machine. After about thirty-five minutes, a petite woman comes downstairs, enters the waiting room and explains she is just finishing with another couple.

Me, "I am confused."

Her, "What are you confused about?"

Me, "I'm confused because our appointment was scheduled for 3 p.m. and we've been waiting here for over a half hour."

Her, "If you notice, I don't have any clocks in the waiting room. It's all part of the experience. I am finishing up. I appreciate you."

She then tells us to look through the book on the endtable, and puts allegedly relaxing music on at a volume that is very unrelaxing.

I am not sure what to say.

She then walks over to her phone, looks at it, sets it back down and walks away to return to her clients. Although I am irritated, I kind of like her energy and think she is kinda Kumbaya, and a bit like me.

I look through the book filled with testimonials from clients about how great Melissa is, and how her greatness transcends and only enhances her skills as a masseuse. I am slightly intrigued yet still hot, frustrated, and bored.

Now both of us are taking turns looking out the window to check the status of the car. After ten more minutes, yet another kid walks in. This time it's a girl, a toddler holding a stick that must have once held a fake flower judging from the medical adhesive tape still around it. Moments later an older boy, a teenager, enters the room to grab the toddler. He apologizes to us and asks if we have read the book on the endtable. I confirm, and he says, "Wait until you see the one upstairs."

At this point, we have been waiting in the tiny room with no AC for almost an hour. We decide this is BS. Just as my boyfriend begins to call AMEX to initiate a refund, Melissa comes downstairs and says she is ready for us. We are ushered upstairs to a room with a couch, one massage table and, lo and behold, this room has an AC unit.

Melissa, "I appreciate you. I have been working since 7 a.m. and you know how when one person is late blah, blah, blah. I appreciate you and want to repair any damage I have done to our relationship and really want you to have a wonderful experience."

Holy Tony Robbins!

Me, "Melissa, I appreciate what you've said. I just have to let you know that creating a wonderful experience after you start the experience off in such a negative way is very challenging, as some of us do care about time and, by the way, this is

supposed to be a couple's massage but there is only one of you."
I say this, gently feeling her Namaste energy.

Melissa, "It's all part of the experience. I appreciate you."

So apparently, I am supposed to watch my middle-aged boyfriend get massaged by Melissa and somehow really enjoy the experience. As much as I love my boyfriend, I am not so much appreciating Melissa about now.

Melissa leaves the room and we determine my boyfriend will go first. I decide that once she starts the massage, I will lie on the couch and do a body scan meditation. We both look at each other upon realizing there's a strange noise that sounds like an icemaker. When I turn to look, it's just the sound coming from a little speaker. It's supposed to be the soothing sounds of a thunderstorm.

Melissa enters the room and I close my eyes to begin my mindfulness meditation. I am starting to relax from the annoying wait, however the music changes and now it's supposed to sound like rain with tree branches rustling except it sounds like rain and bacon frying. With mindfulness meditation, we are supposed to focus on our breath and not attach to thought, so basically I had a Bacon Meditation.

After focusing on bacon for a while, I was finally able to focus on my breath and went into deep relaxation. Forty-five minutes later, I sat up on the couch and watched Melissa massage my boyfriend and again, while I love him, watching him get a massage was *meh*. Finally, it was my turn. Since it was an unconventional situation and the appreciative masseuse spoke English, I decided to take the opportunity to talk the entire time because that's what I do, and my boyfriend could be included in the experience and not have such a *meh* experience watching me get massaged.

We had a nice conversation. I learned quite a bit about Melissa's life and she said some lovely things including, "I appreciate you," many more times.

Melissa, "There's a reason why you are here."

Me, "Okay, please tell me more."

Melissa, "Maybe to think about time a little more."

After much conversation and "Shelley, we are sisters from another mother," at the end of the massage, Melissa said, "I appreciate you and will be bounding up the stairs to read what you wrote in my book. I appreciate you and we'll definitely keep in touch. I appreciate you."

I wrote something lovely in her book and after close to three hours, we left. I texted her to thank her, she never responded. I appreciate you.

CHAPTER 8

Ctrl + Alt + Petite

I am a little person. No, not a little person, as in the PC way to refer to a dwarf. And, no, I am not a child. I am, however, someone people refer to as "little," often "tiny," sometimes "small," and more appropriately, "petite."

I haven't changed size much over the years and honestly don't remember being referred to by the above-mentioned adjectives throughout my life as much as I do now.

I never thought of myself as being a little person, and although I come from short people, it just so happens that I am the tallest female in my family. I am certainly taller than an Oompa Loompa, Munchkin, or Smurf. I do, however, know that as we age, we get shorter while our ears and feet grow. Therefore, I will likely be a hobbit in my later years, or perhaps Gollum because I am "little, "tiny," and "petite."

People often tell me things like, "I wish I was that petite," or "I haven't been that small since I was twelve."

It's funny, though, because again I never thought of myself as tiny, maybe because I'm loud. And that's because I'm Jewish. Okay, maybe that's not why, but somehow I equate the ability to project my voice in a verbose way as being larger than life (aka tall), and I have always been strong. Yet as I get older, the number of times I hear how tiny I am has increased exponentially. Recent examples of said references include the following.

Email received after meeting my new boss for the first time a couple weeks ago included the following, "Shelley, it was great to meet you. Blah, blah blah and you are a *tiny unique lady.*"

Boyfriend after purchasing a new cosmetics case, "You can pack all your *tiny* little dresses in there for the move."

Baltimore shop owner, "No, we don't carry XS. You are so *tiny.*"

In the early nineties, although petite, I was also sophisticated, as evidenced by the diminutive pantsuits I purchased from a little retail boutique easily found in local malls, Petite Sophisticate. The circular clothing rounds were a dream-filled wheel of suits in any color to match whatever season you are. Back in the day, people actually had color consultants do a color analysis, and those particular colors would relate to a particular season. I'm a winter.

At a time when its clothes were only half as slutty as they are now, I could also go across the mall to Bebe to buy an itty bitty skirt. Around the same time when I was almost effort-lessly able to purchase clothes and look sophisticated while wearing them, I was also able to wear really high heels, which may have helped offset the appearance of tininess. Therefore, I was a much taller sophisticated or half-slutty version of myself.

Holy conundrum, people! It is very challenging to find *tiny* clothes, especially *tiny* age-appropriate yet artsy clothes. You may offer suggestions, and I will simply reply, "Thank you," as I know pretty much all the places in the country (and online) to purchase petites, and I have one word—fugly. Yes, I know I could buy larger sizes and have alterations made, but that's not the point. It's like the country went Ctrl + Alt + Petite.

Hypothesis: If I find some *tiny* clothes and wear really high heels, I will appear less *tiny*.

Outcome: False.

Shoe shopping now presents an entirely new set of challenges. Apparently the circumference of my feet is smaller than the average person's, and therefore most uppers (the part of the shoe that goes over your foot) are too large. No, narrow doesn't solve the problem; it's a problem with the girth, not the width.

I just ordered two relatively inexpensive linen dresses on Etsy from a dressmaker in Lithuania. She carries XXS and even asked for my measurements. I will let you know the outcome. If that doesn't work, I can always use clothespins and stand against a wall as well as duct tape my neck, but that's a story for another day.

Ctrl + Alt + Complete.

CHAPTER 9

Cute biker guy

I was racing to get a few things done. The unceasing adrenaline buzz of stress that begins coursing through my body the minute I start my workday was in full force. I had to get there. There was no way I was going to cancel.

I was now running late. I threw my helmet on, went downstairs, grabbed my bike and left the building like a bat out of hell. Okay, not sure at fifty-three years-old anyone but me would describe me that way. Any rodent with wings, I turned the corner, stopped at a stoplight where I typically hover with my feet still on the pedals, but the light was too long so I had to dismount but not without exposing my panties due to the dress being stuck on the end of the seat.

Me to cute biker guy behind me, "Excuse the panty shot."

Cute biker guy behind me, "I like your tattoo."

It's rush hour, which means all intersections are blocked due to cars racing through the yellow yet still unable to make it across the intersection. Cute biker guy goes ahead of me and I feel safe weaving through cars behind him until the next stoplight brings us to halt. No panty shot this time.

Me to cute biker guy, "I am going to see a friend I haven't seen in over thirty years!"

Cute biker guy, "I am going to see my therapist."

Light turns green and I'm again weaving through cars behind him as he knocks on a cab trying to turn left in front of him. It's like an arcade game, in a real life dangerous sort of way. We hit yet another stoplight.

Me to cute biker guy, "You don't need a therapist. You're a lifesaver! You're helping a stranger get to her destination unscathed. You are altruistic and giving."

Cute biker guy, "I always pick the wrong women."

Red light turns green. I'm right behind him. My hero, he's guiding me along the narrow path between the two lanes. Another stop.

Me to cute biker guy, "If I were younger, I would have a big crush on you and you would like me. I'm artsy and kind of crazy, but I am not an addict and don't do anything in excess."

Light turns green. We ride over the Michigan Avenue bridge.

Cute biker guy, "You only want me for sex."

Me to cute biker guy, "I probably need to go to the therapist instead. I am always objectifying men and putting my expectations on them to completely conform to the norms of society."

Cute biker guy, "I'm going to therapy."

Me to cute biker guy, "Thank you for getting me to my destination safely. I love you."

Cute biker guy, "I love you, too."

I parked my bike, run into the hotel bar, and there she is. I can't even believe it, thirty-five years! I throw my arms around her, thrilled she reached out to me to let me know she was in town.

We spent the next thirty to forty minutes as if no time had passed catching up on each other's journeys and walking down memory lane. We then said goodbye. I hope we see each other again soon.

I threw on my helmet and rode back home to do a little more work. No stress buzz, just a warm feeling in my heart and a smile on my face.

"Let's keep this brief"

CHAPTER 10

Dear Santa

I feel a little naughty. No, not that kind of naughty. You see, I've been feeling kind of bitchy and down when the fact of the matter is I am very blessed and have a lot more than other people.

Santa, I have been a little lonely, as you know because you are Santa. I work at home in my hovel and it's isolating. So the thing is, Santa, I have been naughty because I feel like a user. I have been using this woman. The problem is she has really bad breath, kind of like a mix of garbage and bad wine.

Santa, I'm not proud of it. I am not using her because she has bad breath; I am using her because I would really prefer not to be around her and her breath but sometimes when I have nothing to do after work and want to be around someone, I text this woman to see what she is doing so I don't have to be alone.

Any halitosis, here is what always happens. I meet up with her usually in the Viagra Triangle, because that's where she likes to go. I either have a soda water or a glass of wine. Santa, it's like I have short-term memory because as soon as that breath hits me, I recoil and remember this really is a terribly unpleasant idea.

Any doing the same thing and expecting different results, besides the breath thing, she elbows me when she talks. You know, like the, "You get it?" kind of elbowing.

Santa, this isn't working for me. Last time I saw her, I had a very distasteful reminder of her breath and she seemed to be elbowing more than usual. I finally got fed up and said, "If you elbow me one more time, I am going to hit you."

Any empty threat, Santa, I'm really sorry. It's very unbecoming for anyone let alone for a woman of my age to threaten to hit someone.

Santa, for Christmas, may I please be a minty nice person with minty fresh friends?

Love,
Shelley

CHAPTER 11

Deep tissue

"They give a happy ending," she said.

"Oh, my good God, really?" I exclaimed with a look of faux shock and awe on my face.

So there is a well-known person, who shall remain nameless, staying in an extended stay suite in my building. I have a huge pretend crush on him, partly because he is hot and partly because he is older than the average angst-ridden thirty-something-year-old tenant whose rent is paid from an account on the North Shore.

Any Hollywood, often times I have seen Mr. Well Known Person after he has just come from a massage. He always says the same thing "Ahhh, I just came from Massage-O-Rama (not the real name) and I am so relaxed. Ahhh . . . deep tissue, ahh . . . " Something to that effect.

Well, I've been to Massage-O-Rama and have never had a worse massage in my life. The massage therapist basically pet me like a puppy. You know that quizzical expression you make with one side of your lip curled up and eyes squinted? Well, imagine me naked, face down, with this expression on my face as a spider crawls on the floor beneath the face cradle.

So this weekend, I had a massage elsewhere and inquired with this massage therapist about Massage-O-Rama. That's when she told me, "They give a happy ending."

I thought to myself, "Ahhh . . . deep tissue."

Any handholding, I ran into another famous person this weekend. He is locally famous but not in a good way. This guy, the Hair Replacement Cowboy who shall also remain nameless, is just plain creepy. He sits in the park in the Viagra Triangle with his Red Harley Road King tour bike that everyone knows has never toured unless you call a five-block radius a tour. He is about seventy-five with long blonde hair, wears a cowboy hat, leather pants and a leather vest with no shirt underneath. He is like some sort of man-prune.

Back in the seventies this guy drove around in his yellow Excalibur for hours wearing the exact same creepy cowboy outfit. I imagine he drove in circles every night, I don't know, perhaps looking for bald in all the wrong places?

Mr. Hair Replacement Cowboy tries to talk to me from time to time. Apparently, back in the day, he was famous for doing really good toupees and stuff. He still carries around a portfolio of his work. Holy Hair Club for Men! All I can think of is that it's 2014, and the men in those photos look like they were in either a Prell or Brylcream commercial before they succumbed to the terrible hairloss that drove them to toupees and photos that are, quite frankly, uncomfortable.

Every time I see Mr. Hair Replacement Cowboy, if he catches me unaware, he reintroduces himself as if he had just woken up after three decades and doesn't quite know where he is. I'm in the park yesterday and he walks through with this young woman and, oh crap, he stops and tries to shake my hand and predictably starts to reintroduce himself to me. He probably wants to make me a hairpiece. Did my mom, who's always complaining about my hair being too short, tell him where to find me?

I said, "I know who you are. I've known who you are for like ever, and may I suggest you might want to put on a shirt."

As if I am not grossed out enough, he says "Don't you like it? It's sort of kinky."

Any heebie-jeebies, I bet he goes to Massage-O-Rama.

Ahhh . . . deep tissue.

"Daddy Issues"

Dad. larger than life. Doesn't look anything like my hippie dad!

me - so lonely! Sad ¨

PUGS! Nuff said!

Even the dog doesn't want to be with me.

Food keeps me Company

CHAPTER 12

Does this marathon make me look fat?

It was 2001. Exactly one year and three days after quitting my habit of smoking a pack a day of true cowboy killers, Marlboro Reds. I smoked for years. I loved smoking. In high school we actually had a smoking lounge. I even smoked on airplanes on the way to college in upstate New York. I once smoked on a horse. Why? The opportunity just happen to present itself and I just happen to atop a western saddle and it just seemed right.

I actually met my ex-husband because of smoking. He lived across the hall from me. Shortly after I moved in, I saw him in the hallway and could detect the faint smell smoke emanating from him.

Me, "Do you smoke?"

Him (paraphrasing), "Why, yes. Yes, I do."

Me, "I smoke too, but I don't smoke in my apartment."

Him, "You can come over any time you want to smoke."

Me, "Okay. And after that we can go on our first date, become friends with benefits, run across the hall naked to each other's apartment, and you'll have to walk around the circumference of my freshly vacuumed rug. Then we can break up and I can hear you having sex with someone else because, after all, you are right across the hall and then we can fall in love for real, get married, you can hate my mother, we can get divorced and why not get sued by our landlord while we are at it."

Him, "Okay."

Any happily ever after ending three years later, I decided to quit smoking and run a marathon.

Okay, it wasn't that simple. I got a job offer for a company based in California, and learned I would be going out west for three weeks of training. I thought no one in California smoked, because California was really the first state to banish smoking in restaurants.

I threw on the nicotine patch after an ill-fated attempt a few years earlier when the doctor accidently wrote me a script for the estrogen patch and I left the drugstore with a carton of smokes.

After only a day in California, I soon realized some people actually do smoke in California, but they definitely didn't wear Ann Taylor suits. Holy harsh hemline lesson!

I had never been a runner, and actually started running 5Ks a few months before I quit smoking. It was fun. I'd finish running, hack up a lung, and my boyfriend who later became my husband would meet me with Starbucks and my smokes. I would proudly strut back home with my race bib still pinned on and a cigarette dangling from my mouth. Prior to that, I did work out all the time, and mostly partook of the Stairmaster, hanging on for dear life after setting it on the highest level to ensure I burned the most calories. Any anorexic tendencies, I always showered before going to the gym in order to hide the cigarette smell.

I loved training for my first marathon. I loved the camaraderie of my training group and the friends I made in my running group. I literally loved running. It came easy to me. I loved each milestone run and would exclaim, "This is the longest I have ever run my life."

I also loved singing while running.

So here it was. Marathon morning.

I hardly slept the night before. Not because of nerves but because I had been bleaching my teeth for my upcoming wedding and the bleach caused these crazy zappy shocks that kept me awake through the night. My teeth were now as white as Chiclets, but hey you can never be too thin, too rich or have white enough teeth. If you ever want to see the results, I'll send you some of my wedding photos where I am straining to get the most teeth visibility possible. I look like I'm either in pain or have to take a really big sh...vow.

The entire marathon experience was magic. It was all energy, nerves, and excitement. I can't even explain it. It was extraordinary. I had my name on my shirt and would smile every time I heard, "Go, Shelley, go."

It was nothing less than mesmerizing. So many friends came out to cheer me on, my then fiancé had a poster made and it was hanging in our living room window. Our living room faced the street, right on the marathon course. He was out there with our dogs and ran over to hug me. The last few miles were brutal, but I made it.

My mom and dad were waiting for me and I was so exhausted, elated and proud, however, my fiancé was nowhere to be found. Turns out he couldn't find our designated meeting place, the Chicago Area Runners Tent, and decided to go home. That's an entirely different story in itself, resulting in me limping away from home, sitting at a diner by myself, crying with my medal on, and then limping to the park where I cried some more.

I finally went home, we did get married, he did hate my mother, we did get divorced, and we were subsequently sued by our landlord for allegedly breaking our lease. I ended up running twenty more marathons, six ultra marathons, and countless halves.

I don't run marathons anymore after a lumbar fusion. I hug my ex-husband when I see him. I feel blessed to have been able to run so many races, train with so many awesome friends in Chicago and North Carolina . . .

The days leading up to the marathon are bittersweet but I will be out there clapping just as you did for me.

CHAPTER 13

Does this telephone make me look old?

"Let me curl up on the couch for a nice Zoom with my friend Sarah," said nobody. Okay, maybe someone with a friend named Sarah somewhere once said it.

When I want to call my friend Sarah, she doesn't require an appointment and, as matter of fact, clothing is optional. I just curl up on the couch next to my dog, River, who seems to enjoy the fact that I'm no longer arting at the counter and can now be physically close to him. If Sarah's available, she will probably answer, and if not, she'll probably call me back.

Okay, sure I want to get nostalgic and talk about telephones. I can still remember my childhood phone number even though it's been forty years since I've had to use it.

I remember the ladies with nice voices who answered, "Directory Assistance, how may I help you?" I remember walking from room to room to see which phone was off the hook as evidenced by a sound that was almost as annoying as the clappy hold music at your doctor's office.

"Thanks for the memories, Shelley," I hear you thinking to yourself.

"You're welcome," I think back at you.

"Not the clappy one," you think.

"I got you," I think back.

I want to drive us back down the forgotten roads of, "At the tone the time will be . . ." and tell you how I used to imitate that voice so well, I was asked by many a friend to please call so-and-so and do that impression for them. Okay, maybe only one friend and, who knows, she may be the same friend who can't wait to curl up on the couch for a good Zoom with her friend Sarah.

How about the things we don't hear anymore? Such as:

"Get off my line."

"Do you know how much that will cost? That's a toll call."

"Use the phone book."

When was the last time you heard the crash of a receiver? That's a memory I don't want to relive.

I've realized, and maybe you have too, that in a world that can feel as noisy and tangled as an old phone cord, and sometimes as hard, inviting gentleness into my life feels extra good, inviting quiet into my life feels extra better, inviting intimacy into my relationships feels really nourishing. And cultivating joy? Well, that's my jam!

There is joy in a phone call with no appointment required, no calendar confusions, and no thinking about time zones. I have an eighty-four year-old mother who lives across the country, and our relationship has never felt better. While we do email and I send her my art of the day, to hear her voice on the other end of the phone, maybe the first voice I ever heard and probably the first voice to say my name, is definitely worthy of a couch curl up.

I really try to give good phone, and by this I mean give you my full presence, and at least tell you if I'm unable to do so. Try me! And by the way, you will rarely, if ever, get a busy signal, however, I may fake you out with a very precise rendition of, "The number you have reached has been disconnected. The new number is 555-555-5555. Please make a note of it," which you will never do because Sarah's number has been embedded in your brain for years.

Friendship equals no appointment required.

"Does this phone make me look old?"

CHAPTER 14

Don't smoke

Most people don't know I'm a former smoker. No, not *that* kind of smoker—a girl who smokes only when she drinks. I mean I was a full-fledged Marlboro Red, cowboy killer pack-a-day smoker.

I started smoking in high school. We had a twenty-by-twenty-foot graffiti-filled stinky, nasty, dirty smoking lounge where us teenagers were free to light up between class, during free period, after lunch, or when cutting class. I don't totally understand how one could cut class in a high school with only a hundred students and spend the time in the smoking lounge without getting busted.

The other kind of smoking was not done in the smoking lounge. The other kind of smoking was done in walking class, a form of P.E. we could take because our very expensive private school had one tiny gym shared by the entire school from kindergarten to us teenage smokers, hence walking class, or walk and smoke class, if you will.

So yes, I was a smoker in the days when smoking was not so taboo. I smoked on a plane, on a horse, and pretty much everywhere. I ran my first 5K and my ex-husband greeted me with a Starbucks and my smokes. I proudly walked down the street coughing, smoking, and drinking coffee with my race number pinned to my shirt.

Cigarettes is how I met my ex. I met him directly across the hall after just moving in and asked if he smoked. "Yes," he said, and the rest is a very brief history.

The best part of smoking was that sex would last longer because you took a smoke break. The worst part of smoking was that I was kind of OCD. Before leaving my apartment, I always flushed any cigarette butts down the toilet, physically watching the water rinse the stubs away. And yet, when leaving the apartment, I'd walk to the elevator, turn around, walk back to the apartment, open the door and look in the bathroom to see if my cigarette butts somehow magically erupted back out of the toilet totally dry, reignite themselves, and cause a massive fire that would burn down all my shitty, stinky smokey stuff. I swear sometimes I would check three times, the entire process, walk to the elevator, back to the apartment, and check the bathroom. Seriously cray-cray!

When I quit smoking, I think I just checked to see if the door was locked two or three times, back and forth, to and from the elevator or stairs, depending where I lived at the time.

FYI to you smokers, a year and three days after quitting, I ran my first marathon, which was part of the reason for the divorce from the guy I met because of smoking—that is an entirely different WG story although he is featured in the next paragraph. Not that marathons or quitting smoking cause divorce, nor does smoking get you a husband. I'm just saying that if I can quit smoking and run marathons, so can you.

I don't know when I grew out of the checking for cigarette butts, but there is one thing I haven't grown out of yet, and maybe you can relate. I'm a total non-closer. I can't seem to learn my lesson.

I thought about it yesterday when an avalanche of blue-berries came pouring out of the fridge like little blue pebbles being shot at me from the plastic container I failed to close. Not only did they attack me, but some fell behind the produce bin. Now, that's not such a bad non-closer incident. It's when you have the good old oil and vinegar salad dressing non-closer incident. It's almost impossible to clean that up. It goes everywhere, under the fridge, in all the drawers, on everything. Weeks later, you still find oily carp when you thought you cleaned up everything. It takes something like a hundred sheets of wet soapy paper towels for that kind of non-closer incident.

Lucky for me, I am a paper towel hoarder, primed and ready for my non-closer incidents. My former husband was constantly dealing with my non-closer issues, endless surprises of dropped and broken jars of stuff I didn't close.

Him, "Shelley, you never close anything."

Me, "Oops."

Recently, I had a major non-closer spillage of medication I use to help me sleep and River, my forever dog, happened to get a tiny piece of a broken pill while I was trying my best to quickly pick up all the pills. Alas, not quick enough. About thirty minutes later, he couldn't keep his poor little head up, and had no idea why. He kept looking at me and then his little head would fall, and then he would raise it again and it would fall down again. Don't worry. I checked online to make sure he would be okay.

So, my non-closer issues inadvertently caused my dog to be drugged. You'd think I would learn but you would be wrong, as now one of the rugs has a nice purple stain from a wayward blueberry crushed under foot that not even the power of a Tide Stain Stick can handle.

In keeping with the theme of this weird story, I really don't have any idea how to close this other than to say that maybe if I had actually closed the lid on the toilet... okay, never mind.

Don't smoke!

" Sex, Romance, Takeout "

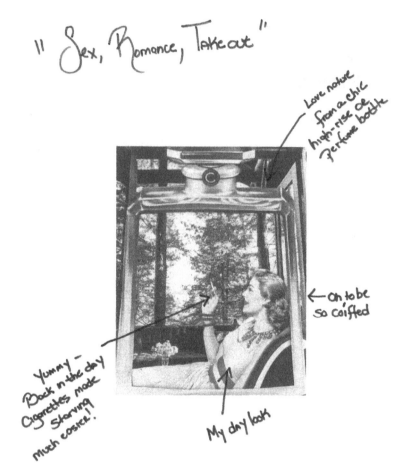

Love nature
from a chic
high-rise or
Perfume bottle

← Oh to be
so coifed

Yummy –
Back in the day
cigarettes made
starving
much easier!!

My day look

CHAPTER 15

Driving with my mom

I have owned a car for a total of six years in my entire life. I really didn't want to learn how to drive, and thought merging was essentially all luck. I thought about what was behind my desire to not learn to drive and since it's easiest to blame things on your parents, I decided to blame my mom.

My mom's driving was a rollercoaster trip to the dark side. Getting in the car with her was an act of courage, like walking the plank. She seemed to simultaneously put her makeup on, drop something and look for it under the seat while digging through her purse for a piece of gum and beeping the horn at the guy she just swerved into as well as using the median as a motor vehicle centering devise, you know, like a bumper car track. She was like an octopus doing eight things all the while what I would loosely call driving. Thank the good God texting wasn't a thing during my youth.

And by the way, this is not at all to say my driving skills are so superior. After all, I did drive the car into the side of the house.

How about you?

CHAPTER 16

Eva's room

"When you're down on the ground, cocaine! She don't lie, she don't lie she don't lie...cocaine!"

I strummed and sang, strummed and sang. It was 1977, baby! Yeah!

Okay, I had no idea what cocaine was and why she didn't lie. It would be decades before I knew. I don't even know what came first in terms of my own knowledge, Eric Clapton or "Cocaine." I think Eric Clapton. I don't lie, I don't lie, I don't lie...okay!

I was fourteen years-old, singing and strumming away on my six-string acoustic guitar to the songs of the sixties and seventies limited to the aforementioned "Cocaine," "Leaving on a Jet Plane," and "House of the Rising Sun." I had no idea Lola was a man and someone else was glad they were a man. I always tell people, "I've been to that desert. I've been on that horse and he did have a name, I just was never allowed to tell anyone."

Don't even try it! I don't tell, I don't tell, I don't tell . . . No Name!

The reason I wanted to take guitar lessons was due to a girl-crush I had on a beautiful teen named Andy when I was eleven or twelve years-old. She was fourteen and I thought she was everything—popular, pretty teeth, and she was *developed*. I was sure she even wore a bra to hold her recently developed breasts. At eleven, I was obsessed with wanting to develop and the whole, "Are you there, God, it's me, Margaret," thing.

Not only was Andy perfect to me, she also played guitar! We sat in a circle on the cabin floor while Andy strummed and played Simon & Garfunkel's 59th Street Bridge Song. *"Slow down, you move too fast..."*

I wanted to be Andy. "Mom, I want to take guitar lessons."

Good thing my mom was friends with Andy's mom.

I learned the 59th Street Bridge Song. It was easy. C, G, A Minor 7, D, C, G, A Minor 7, D, so on and so forth. But I was nothing like Andy. A hippy guitar teacher wasn't going to help this prepubescent, angst-ridden, chubby unhappy kid whose mom started dying her hair because she wanted her to remain blonde but instead turned her hair the color of a copper kettle. However, I did get to play in front of many audiences. Some of the crowd faves included the TV theme from "Welcome Back Kotter," and "Sunshine on My Shoulders." So what if the audience consisted of many other prepubescent, angst-ridden, chubby unhappy kids?

Shortly after learning "Cocaine," developing but still angst-ridden, I traded in my guitar for a piano for the sole purpose of learning Beethoven's Für Elise, not without many stops beforehand including a stint as the oldest student and the only Jew required to play "Oh, Little Town of Bethlehem," in Mrs. Smelly Cat Pee Piano Teacher's basement. Not long after that came I don't play, I don't play, I don't play...PAIN.

Not physical pain, emotional pain. I am no longer a child. I'm a teen and I am ugly, I am fat, I am lonely, I have no friends, my sister locks herself in her room, my mom and dad are never around, completely oblivious to cocaine, pain . . . insane.

I am a latchkey kid who gets relentlessly teased every day at school. I want to die. I try to overdose on four aspirin.

I am in Eva's room. Eva used to be our live-in, and wore the exact same uniform as Alice from the Brady Bunch. When she was mad, she exclaimed, "Sheet!"

I was her favorite, although she did get mad at me once when I tossed my slice of bread with peanut butter into the street cuz I saw the Good Humor Man.

Eva was gone. No one was around. Eva's room is where I took guitar lessons, sang and strummed. Eva's room is where I practiced Für Elise.

Eva's room is where I am with different boys who don't want anyone to know they are with me.

CHAPTER 17

Exhaust-A-Dog

If you love me and I'm feeling sad, please buy me paper towels, preferably Bounty in a six-pack or greater. Having a cabinet full of paper towels gives me a feeling of abundance, so please do this for me if you love me. Won't you? Paper towels equals happy Weird Girl.

Potato, my short-term rescue doe, went to doggy daycare, which should really be called Exhaust-A-Dog. It was a huge blessing for both of us today. Early this morning I walked downtown to Target to feed my paper towel addiction, and had a manicure during my lunch break. I don't think I have ever done that pre-Potato. There was peace and quiet there except for the TV. I don't have TV anymore. Not because I think I am too cool or oh, so literary. The truth of the matter is I am fragile. Actually, the real truth of the matter is I had a little *problem*, or shall we call it an *opportunity*.

I have faced major adversity over the last few years and there was a time when I couldn't watch anything that would trigger fear. This eliminated the news and many other shows, including some sitcoms which scared the crap out of me because they were so stupid.

You know how there is comfort in familiarity? Well, my *problem,* or opportunity, is that during this fearful time in my life, I became addicted to the Real Housewives shows on Bravo. These shows and people with their predictable fucked-up-ness and dysfunction were really a comfort to me. I found myself watching all of them. Oh, holy judgmentalness. Judge not, lest you be judged!

Any housewives, I watched all of them including Atlanta, Beverly Hills, New York, New Jersey, and I am here to tell you, these crazy bitches got me through some of the worst days of my life. When my life started getting better and I moved back to Chicago, my need for the Housewives began to diminish because I started having real relationships, and while some of them have scared the crap out of me, I no longer had to cuddle up to Nee Nee, and so and so. Crap, I blocked out their names.

Any mental block, I don't need them anymore. Now the boatload of money I save on cable can be put towards Exhaust-A-Dog.

CHAPTER 18

False eyelashes
feminism & fascination

The familiar pervasive smell of Norrell perfume and cigarettes wafted in the air as I sat on the floor watching Captain
Kangaroo and eating my Quisp Cereal. Click, clack, went the
staccato sound of her Joseph's Salon of Shoes platforms as she
scurried around the house in a hurry to leave. A dark brown
pinstriped suit (I guess you would call it that, even though it
was a blazer with matching hot pants) was her de rigueur
attire. Perfectly coiffed brunette bun hairpiece and ringlets
framing her face, false eyelashes and blue eye shadow with just
a slip of black eyeliner. She was fascinating.

She was my mother.

My mother was glamour, brains and balls. A warrior of
the late sixties, she was armed with a briefcase, a Parliament
cigarette between perfectly manicured fingers, and tireless

ambition. She flew across the country habitually mistaken for a stewardess, and was soon kicked out of the ladies Mahjong club for not giving it enough personal attention.

I didn't know anyone like her. She was captivating, fascinating, frightening and compelling. My friends' moms were apron-wearing, cookie baking, snack serving clones of Mrs. Brady.

Mrs. Brown, my mom, was an anomaly, a force of nature, larger than life at all of five feet (five-foot-five in heels).

My mom wrote a book, invented the Furniture Fashion Show, and started a mail-order microwave cookware business with a retail shop to follow (yes, I was a victim of many unsuccessful attempts to actually brown a chicken in that thing).

Mom was on Phil Donahue and the Oprah Winfrey show. She was a national spokeswoman for Armstrong and Whirlpool. I could go on and on about her myriad of pursuits and accomplishments.

I thought I wanted a Mrs. Brady mom, but my mom was a star with more chutzpah than anyone I have ever met in life. She is smart, funny, fashionable and has more stories than anyone I know. It actually took me time to catch up to her computer agility.

Growing up with a feminist mother was confusing and, at times, felt simply abnormal. But if my mom wasn't who she was, I wouldn't be who I am. As matter of fact, women like my mother were the pioneers who taught many of us perseverance and endurance. She didn't have to burn her bra or participate in any sort of demonstration. She just had to stay true to herself, no more hot pants. Now armed with an iPad and a roster of clients who still use her as a publicist, she remains larger than life.

She is my hero.

"Butterflies of New York"

My mom always called me here Butterfly

I love nature from the 25th floor of an urban highrise

This is called a "Radio" go ask your Grandma!

As if I would be caught dead in public in a bathing suit!

CHAPTER 19

Fast walker

Besides having a low, loud voice, I am also a fast walker, in a race to nowhere in particular. I am probably more punctual than most everyone. In fact, I can be overpunctual, forcing me into an unnecessary self-inflicted hold music prison while being much too early for a conference call, or waiting in an empty theatre for the movie to begin because I think everyone wants to do what I want to do, and I fear ending up with a first row seat and a neck strain.

Any Intergalactic Planetary (I just felt like writing that). Any random, free-flowing stream of consciousness, reeling it back in, when people are walking too slow, I have to get in front of them. I often find myself unnecessarily jogging in mid-height heels (not the high ones from days of yore because they require a taxi, not a fast walk) to get in front of them for no reason at all. I am sure no one is paying attention but I can only imagine if they were, it could be quite an unusual sight to see this petite and stunningly beautiful woman doing a little jog just to get in front, and continue fast walking to nowhere.

Any stride-right, when I was a pre-spinal fusion runner, I always had to be at the helm of the group, leading them forward like some Elven Warrior in the Battle of Evermore with true purpose. I simply couldn't run right behind other runners, and would often hear, "Slow down," from the group.

In one running group, there was a woman whom I refer to as the lurker who ran behind me, but not right behind me. The lurker was just off to my left, like a cartoon devil on my shoulder. She never articulated her lurky message, yet maybe she was warning me. I see her once in a while walking down the street, and I just want to jog ahead to get in front of her.

Besides being a low, loud talker and a fast walker, I am a chain breaker. If you send me something to repost because it's going to cure cancer or save someone's life, I will break every chain. I'm sorry that I'm responsible for the continued suffering of so many. I am even more sorry for the pokers left unpoked, and the farmers who somehow need my assistance in Farmville. Maybe the lurker was trying to warn me that I was going to be the cause of so much destruction.

This story really has no end, but I have to run...

CHAPTER 20

Faux grillin'

I suppose it's like an O'Doul's beer, an electric cigarette, or maybe even an Elvis impersonator. You want it to be the real thing, yet it just doesn't quite do it.

I looked at my plate of food and said, "Hey, New York strip, you are a beautiful cut and have sinewy char-like grill lines. Oh, you, yes you, corn on the cobb with your little sporadic darkly browned kernels . . . Oh, don't worry, I see you, little silver-dollar slices of green and yellow squash with your delicate brown searedness."

Well, guess what, you guys? You are all BIG FAKES!

I did all the usual prep. I sliced the squash into little medallions and drizzled the little babies with olive oil and a hint of salt and pepper. I then took the corn and yanked the husk off, thinking the corn has longer hair than me, and then

I took my big hunk of meat, rinsed it off and patted it dry, prepped it with a nice tasty spice rub. Oh, holy grillness, this was going to be awesome! A little feast for little weird me. Okay, I'm ready!

I ran the extension cord out to the balcony and plugged it into my new George Foreman GGR50B indoor-outdoor grill and turned that baby on to number five, the highest number. Yep, cooking with heat! I then went into the tub, excited to relax before my feast. Ahhhhh... the water felt so good, and then Potato started barking at me incessantly. I ignored him, which is what you are supposed to do. So much for the relaxing bath.

It's been a bit of a power struggle over here with my adolescent Puganese. He pretty much hates me, and gives me the death stare whenever I don't do what he wants. However, I hold my ground because I am the alpha here! I can train Potato.

Yep, sure and O'Doul's tastes just like the real thing.

I am a very devoted mom, but let me tell you people, you ask most folks who have ever had a puppy if they went through a period when they asked themselves every day, "What the fuck did I do? My life is now over."

That's where I am right now (non-highrise living puppy parents, I'm afraid you don't count).

Any hot tub, I get out of the bath and I begin placing my food items on the George Foreman GGR50B indoor-outdoor grill. She's a beauty! I time everything perfectly and then put my plate together.

Potato is now pretty much passed out because I walked him for an hour and then brought him to the park where he pretty much wanted to exit the park with everyone but me, especially anyone with a ball.

Potato is now passed out and I have this beautiful meal in front of me. It looks delicious. Everything is cooked perfectly. I take a bite of each item on my plate . . .something's missing.

"You are all fakes!" I yell at my plate.

People, just because it looks grilled doesn't mean it tastes grilled. And just because my puppy is being a willful adolescent doesn't mean he doesn't love me.

My belly is full and my dog is sleeping next to me. He won't always be a puppy and I won't always be faux grilling. Well, maybe just the puppy part is true. Holy hot charcoals, one can hope!

Love,
Shelley

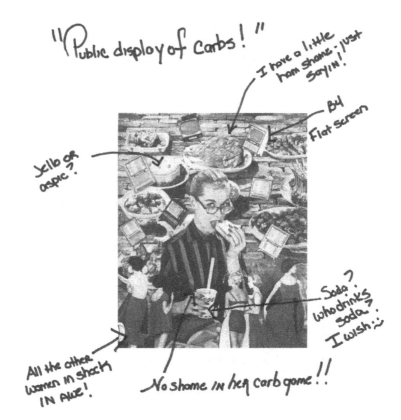

CHAPTER 21

Fifty shades of hoarding

This Weird Girl story is not for the eyes of children under forty. Years before *Fifty Shades of Grey* lived a young woman who looked, talked, and acted identical to me. I will call her Sherry so as not to expose her true identity.

Sherry started dating a very interesting and intriguing man. The man traveled quite a bit and was hardly ever home. The first time Sherry went to his apartment, she thought to herself, "Holy crap! There's a lot of crap in here," but kept it to herself with thoughts of sympathy for this man who was always on the road.

Upon further domain exploration, Shelley, oh crap, I mean Sherry, discovered a padlocked door with a key sticking out from the lock. "Hmmm," she thought for about a second until utter impatience hit, and she asked the man about this room. He didn't say a word as he opened the door. *Holy mother of dungeons,* Sherry almost uttered out loud. The walls were painted red, a red blackout shade covered the window, a variety of whips, chains, belts, stirrups and other who knows what they are called in all sorts of shapes and sizes were hanging from the walls. The room's centerpiece was some kind furniture you will never see in your momma's living room, or any room in your life, for that matter.

Sherry started asking questions but the man really didn't want to talk about it. Several months went by and the man never invited Sherry into that room, nor did he give her any indication of how he used that room.

"Why don't you take me into the room?" she asked.

He would just kind of shrug it off and say something I am not allowed to tell you.

It was only several months after they stopped seeing each other that Sherry realized this man had never thrown away anything he had ever owned in his entire life. A good example—cat food in the pantry. Sherry asked, "Do you have a cat?"

Man, "I used to a few years ago."

Case closed. Sherry realized the man simply no longer used the room, or maybe it was where he was hiding the cat.

CHAPTER 22

First

I had lain on my bed the entire day crying endless tears. The pain was so insidious. It just kept coming in enormous waves. Almost as painful as having to look up the correct grammar for my first sentence in this darn story: The past participle of lie is lain. The past participle of lay is like the past tense, laid.

Holy intense tenses! If you think writing is hard, I'm here to prove it's even harder with all this research I have to do. Any elaboration, the point is that I did not get out of bed all day, and was crying. The only time I got up was to turn the cassette over to the other side, lie back down until the end of the other side, get back up and turn the cassette over. The cassette was "The Best of Bread." Bread had thirteen songs on the Billboard Top 100 chart in the seventies.

This was 1979, and I was sixteen years-old when we met in Florida at Ramblewood, or as my grandmother pronounced it, "Vramblewood" a sprawling senior community near Fort Lauderdale where my Grandma Miriam retired after teaching art in Bayonne, New Jersey.

I loved Nana, my Grandma Miriam. She kept shit real. She wasn't like my other grandma. Nana called me Honey, even when she was angry. Grandma Miriam took a puff of her Raleigh cigarette, which was her smoke of choice until about age ninety, and in her Eastern European mixed with New Jersey dialect said, "Honey is bee shit!"

I dragged on my Marlboro Red and nodded my head in agreement.

That winter, I spent three weeks at Grandma's smoking, drinking coffee, and reading books while the HVAC system was being replaced back home in Chicago. I don't think Grandma Miriam was very happy there. Apparently, senior women are as catty as high school girls, full of gossip and cliques, always fawning over the only two men still alive in the complex. My grandma had something to say about every woman in her posse yet, nonetheless, we went to various earlybird dinners around 4 p.m. where the butter, creamer, sugar, Sweet'n Low, and bread would suddenly disappear from the tabletop and into someone's purse. Not sure if it was first come first steal or what.

I don't know when I first laid eyes on him. I don't even remember how the conversation started, but he was a total fox with reddish curly hair, a bit of a stocky frame, and an east coast dialect. His name was Brad, and he was a sophomore in college at SUNY-Albany. I was a junior in high school. He, too, was there for winter vacation visiting his grandparents, who also called it "Vramblewood." They, too, must have been first generation.

Brad and I started hanging out together. He introduced me to iced tea mixed with orange juice. We went for pizza and even did *it* on the golf course at night, our young bodies silhouetted by the mosquito-filled haze of the distant fluorescent lights. At the end of three weeks, we were telling each other, "I love you."

This was the first boy to ever say those words. Brad was my first love. Leaving Vramblewood was vreally hard!

"Do you know how much our toll bill is?" I'm sure my dad threw in a curse word or two when asking me that question. For younger readers, toll was an additional charge for long distance calling from a landline. In 1979, a rotary phone was how we stayed connected. Brad and I were in love and my heart ached to see him so we schemed up a plan for me to fly out to visit him at SUNY-Albany. We even had a girl from his dorm call my mom on the landline under the pretense I was going to stay with her. Score!

I stayed in his dorm room listening to Michael Jackson's "Off the Wall," on cassette, flipping it from one side to other. This was before we had any sort of speculation about MJ.

Brad would come back to the dorm between classes to bring me a stolen sandwich from the cafeteria. I think we stayed in Albany for two nights. I can't remember for sure, but I do remember going to a party and this really stoned guy talked about polymers for like two hours. We drove to Spring Valley the next day to meet his parents.

One fateful day, not long after the visit, Brad called to tell me, "It's over," due to the distance.

Baby I'm-a want you
Baby I'm-a need you
You're the only one I care enough to hurt about
Maybe I'm-a crazy

Okay, we'll just stop there. The last time I spoke with Brad was right before his wedding. He wanted to see me before tying the knot. Maybe he-a crazy!

CHAPTER 23

Fish S/he

I thought for sure I had killed him/her. His/her lifeless little body was so contorted and odd. I was literally sitting down to write RIP on my Facebook page about him/her.

S/he was very good. Never gave me a problem. Sometimes, s/he was a spaz when I had to do hygiene for him/her, but s/he always calmed down.

The thought of doing harm to a loved one is one thing, but actually killing them, even if by accident, is another. I thought maybe it was a head injury that took him/her down. Thank the good God s/he fought! I didn't know s/he was going to make it.

I'm talking about Galadriel of Lothlorien, my Beta fish who suffers from sexual dysmorphic identity issues due to having a female name, a Tolkien Female Eleven name at that.

I took his/her little square home and gently dumped out the water, as it was time for the weekly cleaning. As always, I have a little bowl where s/he is placed while I am rinsing out his/her tank home, but this time I missed and little Galadriel's cobalt blue body lay on the side of my waterless sink.

I grabbed a plastic spoon, missed him/her, and there s/he was at the precipice of the drain. One slight move and s/he was going down. I quickly took the plastic spoon and scooped him/her up into the bowl that was waterless. I quickly added water from his/her tank that wasn't quite emptied. I cleaned the tank quickly, added purifying drops and put him/her back in there and then *it happened.*

Galadriel went head down to the bottom of his/her little home tank. S/he just laid there. I thought I killed him/her but I started praying really hard and saying, "Come on! Come on, Galadriel!"

S/he started trying to swim but kept going to the bottom again. I thought I was witnessing a slow death.

Well, I didn't kill him/her and maybe just gave him/her brain damage that may help with the sexual dysmorphic identity issues.

CHAPTER 24

Friendship

I love you, friends.

I was standing on top of the toilet trying to pry open the door while looking down at my friend who was stuck in the restaurant bathroom stall while our other friend was using a key to try and jimmy the lock.

She was definitely stuck in there.

Just as I was yanking the door from the top, our friend who was trying to open the door from outside the stall, did the unthinkable—she crawled underneath the stall in one swift, stealthy badass move and opened that bitch of a door to let our friend out. That was one of the boldest friendship moves I've witnessed! Holy biohazard! Our hero was unscathed except for the piece of toilet paper stuck to her shoe as us three exited the bathroom.

Bathroomgate wasn't over just yet. Our hero had left the restaurant for home only to return a few minutes later having realized she didn't have her house keys. We all looked around and I ran to the hostess stand to see if anyone had turned them in. No keys.

I ran past the toilet paper our friend had removed from her shoe to go look in the bathroom. Nope. No keys.

I reported back to our friend, and then we went to ask the bartender whether keys had been turned in. The bartender inquired as to where we thought our friend last had her keys. "Oh yes, yes!" I stated, "She tried to use the keys to jimmy the lock to get our friend out of the bathroom stall!"

The bartender, my friend and I all walked toward the bathroom and on the way, in one stealth swift, badass move, the bartender picked that piece of toilet paper up off the floor with her bare hands, opened the bathroom door, jammed that same hand right into the full bathroom garbage can, and pulled out keys! "Voila!"

She then left the bathroom without washing her hands. Any tabooness, our friend and bathroom diving hero now had her keys.

This little story illustrates the unselfish and sometimes unsavory things people are willing to do for her their friends.

I am so blessed by my friends. The new ones and old ones who have laughed and cried with me, the friends who pick you up when you are so far down you don't think you're going to make it through the shittiest shit times, the friend who loans you her hair for a photo (I was bald, and she swung her long locks over my head), friends who cheered me on during marathons and surgeries, the friends who call me on my shit, the friends who love me just the way I am, and so much more.

I want to thank the friend who went
under that bathroom stall for
reminding me that when you
are a friend, you just do...

"She looks more like her Moother all the time"

I don't mind people telling me I look like my mom as long as she is setting down! She's 5' in heels!

Sometimes you look in the mirror & think "Wow! I look just like my mom!" Other times, "Crap! I look just..."

Nice Manicure

Like "BUTTA"

CHAPTER 25

Gynie

When you are bald but have the ability to grow hair, in order to stay relatively bald, one must go to Supercuts or buy clippers and do it yourself.

Now, I haven't cut my own hair since I was eight when I cut my bangs and apparently invented the asymmetrical hairstyle. Not long after, I was forced into a gum haircut. The kind where you fall asleep with gum in your mouth and when you wake up, you're stuck to your pillow because a wad of gum is completely entangled in your hair. After trying peanut butter and all the other old wife's tales, I took matters into my own hands and cut a big chunk of my hair and then cried because it looked really messed up.

By the way, why isn't it called old husband's tales? I sure know a lot of old husbands who have told me some tales.

Any Hubba Bubba, I love gum. I don't chew it anymore, yet I love it! I especially liked Color Bubbles, not to be confused with Rainblow. I would eat two pieces at a time, chew to get all the sugar coating out of it, throw it out and toss in the next two pieces. It was kind of insane, in fact problematic. Later in life, I switched to Dentyne Fire. That's badass gum that led to a problem with a boyfriend who told me to stop chewing it around him because he said it was like kissing hell.

By far, the best gum for blowing huge badass bubbles was Bazooka. No, no, don't argue with me here. I was an expert and if you want to come over here so I can prove it, you better be packing some. Any Hell Breath, thank the good gum god I still have teeth.

Speaking of teeth, I love going to the dentist. I get giddy excited about having my teeth cleaned. I can honestly say it's one of my favorite things.

Now I can't say the same thing for other types of medical appointments. For instance, the gynecologist. And please, adult women, why do you say, "Gynie?"

It's as though you're putting it in the same realm as a mani-pedi. Going to the gynecologist is not cute. While I love going to the dentist, I don't say I'm going to the Denty.

One time I went to the gynecologist and was kept in the tiny cell of a room in a paper gown with a three-year-old Ladies' Home Journal, with my arms wrapped around my freezing self to keep warm like some imprisoned cray-cray in a padded cell. Picture any Lifetime movie or maybe Saw 3D, but instead of the scary background music, the room was filled with the lovely Muzak version of "Hummingbird Don't Fly Away," played by some sort of flute-like instrument.

Being cold, dressed in paper listening to flute-like Muzak for an hour in a small room got me feeling a little perturbed. Okay, insane. I threw on my clothes and walked out of the room and told the nurse this was unacceptable, that I was leaving, and to tell Dr. Gynecologist (not Gynie) to sit in a small room in a paper gown for an hour and see how he likes it.

Love,

Shelley

"I want to stay in bed & eat cheese. Sew what?"

Wish I knew how to sew! I would make such rockin' stuff

they heavy angst sewing me to the bed

She's smiling I was usually crying- being stuck!

B.L.I. Before Lactose Intolerence

My Mom would be appalled! "Where is your mattress protector!"

CHAPTER 26

How to blow your cool

There is a moment when you just know it, and can't deny it. It's simply the irrefutable truth, and now you have to change the situation because it's no longer working for you. Maybe you come to the realization gradually, or maybe you come to it like a nearly missed red light when you stomp on the brake, and it's right there, unmistakable.

It's the moment when you realize there is only one cool person in the relationship or dating thingy, and it's not the other person.

Was it when he told me I was odd and weird, or asked, "Why do you have those tattoos? What were you thinking?"

Maybe it was when he picked up the entire half of a chicken in a trendy restaurant with his bare hands after asking for ketchup. I am no Queen of Cool, however I think I know uncool. In this day and age, some people blow their cool even before you meet them.

Example A. David (may or may not be his real name), fifty-seven years-old, decided it was sexy to text me, prior to meeting him, a picture of himself in his boxer shorts. Cool blown.

Example B. Steve (quite possibly his real name), fifty-five years-old, decided to tell me, prior to meeting him, that he lied about his age on the dating site. Cool blown.

Example C. Mark, Keith, Dan (all real names) various ages, decided to tell me technically they are not quite divorced. Cool blown times a thousand.

Any Hot Mess, you get it. I am keeping it tame here. I have even received messages containing photos of men's private parts. Okay, not numerous, but more than two. Cool blown!

Yes, married people, this really happens. Even at this stage in my life, people take selfies of their private parts. If you ever notice a woman reach for her phone look at it and recoil, you may think she just got a mean text from a mean girl, but it's probably a photo of a penis from a guy she never met.

Any hung dinger, I consider myself to be fun and I make myself laugh, however sometimes I find myself in a dating thingy realizing that the reason *we* are having fun is because I laugh at everything including the previously mentioned texts. Young women out there, is this something the younger folk enjoy?

Maybe I am dating myself. Maybe I have to literally date myself. Just for accountability purposes, have l blown my cool by getting too attached, by being inflexible and all my other cray-cray...

Have a great day and don't blow your cool!

"Don't let me hear anyone say, 'A little birdie told me.'"

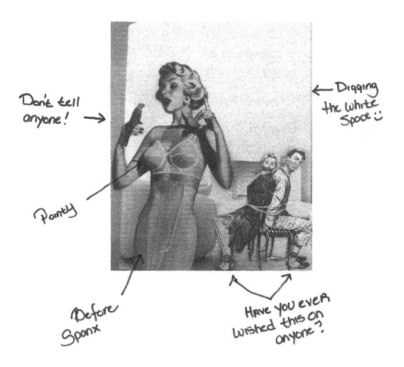

Don't tell anyone! →

← Digging the White Space ∴

Pointy

Before Sponx

Have you ever wished this on anyone?

CHAPTER 27

I come from a shitty hair people

Give me a head with hair, long beautiful hair. Shining, gleaming, streaming, flaxen, waxen. Give me down-to-there hair, shoulder length or longer, here baby, there, momma, ev'rywhere, daddy, daddy.

I thought about this song this morning, knowing I was going to write about my hair. If you remember the song, it's really a hippy dude singing about being a hairy guy, and society's dismay about the statement he was making with freedom to be a guy with long hair.

So I am hair here to say, I come from a shitty hair people. The Browns just don't have good hair. Our hair tends to be thinner, wiry and fly awayish at all times.

Guys tend to like long hair. I have been asked on many occasions, "Have you always had short hair?"

Or, "Why don't you let your hair grow?"

My response has always been, "My people do not have good hair."

I've also been asked, "Have you ever considered breast implants?"

I do not reply with, "I come from a small breasted people."

Any holla back, that's an entirely different Weird Girl story.

So as mentioned yesterday, I was becoming dishwater, the most unattractive adjective for hair. It ranks as high as frizzy, dandruff, alopecia and ingrown.

I did have a Sun-In incident at camp that scarred me for many years. My mom decided she would use some harmless product, I am assuming something akin to Sun-In. I don't think I ever use the word "akin" in daily life, ever. Do you?

Any house music, she would put some crap on my hair once in a while and my hair would be less dishwatery. Ahhh, better living through chemicals.

At some point, I guess the harmless product akin to Sun-In was discontinued and I am assuming my weird mom went directly to the beauty aisle of our neighborhood Jewel-Osco, looked at a box of hair color that she thought would help my straying further and further away from toe/tow headed beginnings.

This is how my hair became the color of a copper kettle and remained that way for several years.

Love,

Shelley

"Message from Society"

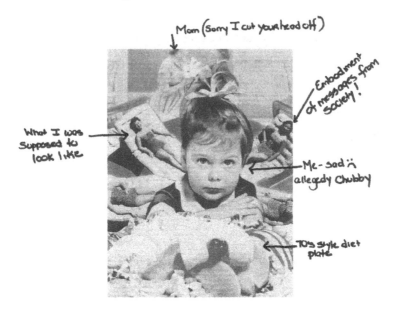

CHAPTER 28

I come from a worried people

I come from a worried people. These people worry and are overly cautious. The worried people are very suggestive and read the side effects on every medication to make sure they experience all of them, even the side effects experienced by the placebo people. If it only happens in males, my female people will figure out a way to have that side effect, too. My people worry out of love, though.

The worried people tell you to go to the doctor when you have a cough because, "You always get Strep throat."

I tell the worried people, "I haven't had Strep since I was fifteen."

The worried people tell me, "Go get a throat culture."

Sometimes I listen to the worried people and get a throat culture so I can ease their worry, and the end result is money spent on copays and sitting in a waiting room with sick people to basically reassure the worried people.

One day I found myself naked in my house with my former boyfriend exclaiming, "What's that on your ass?"

I'm like, "What?"

I quickly go to the bedroom to look in the full-length mirror (no, I didn't lay prone on the bed and no, I didn't have a mirror on the ceiling even though that may have been easier). I assess this thing on my ass. I see a round spot about the size of a quarter with a circular red ring. I turn to my boyfriend and say, "I don't know?"

The next day I remembered a conversation with some people at the gym where I was teaching a spin-abs class. Holy shit! I have *ringworm*, I thought to myself as I compulsively looked at the spot on my ass over and over and over again. These girls at the gym were talking about an outbreak from the mats a few years back.

I go to urgent care, quietly describe my ailment to the receptionist and wait to be seen. I am summoned by a nurse, taken to the exam room, and explain my situation to her as she takes my vitals. A short time later, a redheaded doctor who looks to be about twelve comes into the room and asks if I can pull down my pants so he can take a look. I do as requested, he gets on his knees, moves my ass cheek a little bit and in less than thirty seconds, I am diagnosed with a bruise and given follow-up instructions.

Yes, friends. I come from a worried people and I have inherited the worry gene.

I love you all very much.

Please go to the doctor.

"Rabbits Shouldn't Smoke & Dogs Shouldn't Drive"

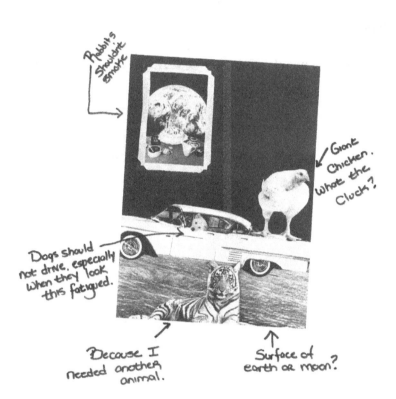

Rabbit's Shouldn't Smoke

Giant Chicken. What the Cluck?

Dogs should not drive, especially when they look this fatigued.

Because I needed another animal.

Surface of earth or moon?

CHAPTER 29

I don't know what to say

"Paaaatty? Paaatty? Paaatteeee?" I shouted in anticipation.

At any moment I knew I would hear "Shelley? Sheelley? Shelleeeee?"

Somehow our voices would inevitably find the way to the source of their plea. Had they not, I would have taken greater measures, however we were soon reunited.

Patty said, "I heard your voice but couldn't tell what direction it was coming from."

We laughed one of those little giggles of faux relief like, "Oh, thank God I found you. I was going to have you paged."

I replied and then practically peed myself because it's 2015, we were on the fifth floor of Bloomies, and the thought of asking a store employee to have Patty paged followed by,

"Patty, please meet your friend in the BCBG department on the fifth floor," heard throughout the store while we both had our cellphones made me fall into a delightful yet immature and inappropriate state of all out hysterics, even more than my interpretive dance while bellowing the lyrics of some seventies Muzak designed to make daytime weekday shoppers feel comfortable, causing them to spend with abandonment, as opposed to the weekend, all music sounding like and including Taylor Swift to make the younger shoppers shop.

"I would climb any mountain. Sail across the stormy..."

Remember when you would get lost and they would page your mom? Folklore has it, my sister once got lost in a store only to be found sitting on a display toilet with her pants down in Sears or some other place like that. Folklore also has it that I somehow fell into Buckingham Fountain and the Fountain at Daily Plaza. I think maybe I was pushed by Lorie Brown.

What am I doing? She wouldn't remember anyway. I'll tell you what she would remember, though. We were very young and my dad took us to one of those mall pet stores. I'm not sure why, because he was a veterinarian. Any utter confoundment, we were by the puppy cages. I was kneeling down petting the cute little puppy in the lowest cage when the puppy in the top cage above decided to go potty...Holy Hair Doo Doo.

For years I recounted that story and replaced the poor victim with my sister. That is, until I was able to own up to my own shit.

Any accountability, reunited, we moved on to a different floor at Bloomingdales while I was still hysterically cracking myself up and tinkling a little over my inner filmstrip, "Lost Woman has friend Paged by Department Store in the Year 2015."

Patty, in shellshock at one of the best bargains I've ever witnessed in my somewhat advanced years and, by the way, shopping years are like dog years but in threes and not sevens, which would make my shopping age . . .

I look at the spidery eye-lashed woman and with faux indignation state, "Where are the deals for people my size?"

She looks at me blankly with tangled lashes and says, "I don't know what to say."

I decided that was the best answer ever in the universe.

When people ask me a direct question, I want to look at them with a blank stare like a slice of Wonder bread with two spiders and state, "I don't know what to say."

After I told Patty a story about Gene Simmons, we parted ways. I had to pee for real at this point. I don't know what say.

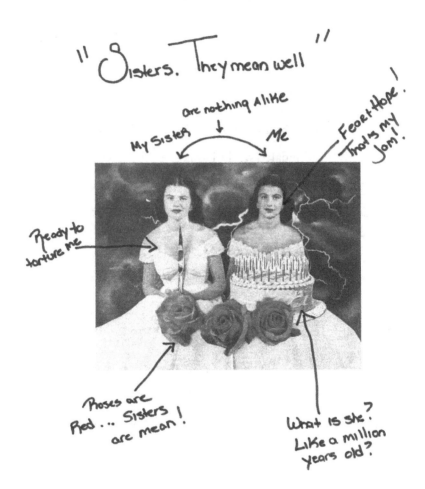

CHAPTER 30

If I can't be a rock star

When I was younger, I wanted to be singer. In fact, I was sure I would become a singer. Like most young girls, my hairbrush was my favorite microphone—and then I started playing guitar.

My first taste of stardom, besides playing and singing in front of my parents' friends in our family room, was at camp, Chippewa Ranch Camp, a Wisconsin camp for bratty spoiled girls from the North Shore. Yes, judgmental, I know and don't care, especially because someone laced my shampoo with Sun-In, a seventies spray-on product that was supposed to give you just a kiss of blonde as if the big ole sun herself had done it, however that fake kiss gave me more like a slap of brassy copper-kettle colored hair. This was at a very vulnerable age—as in puberty, and all the accoutrements that go with it.

That being said, my undeniable musical talents catapulted me into temporary popularity for at least three to five minutes, the length of your average seventies song. I was positioned as the lead guitarist and singer for our cabin's act at the midsummer talent show. I led my cabin mates in a balls-out rockin' song that only I could strum on a six-string nylon acoustic guitar to the theme from, "Welcome Back, Kotter."

> Well, we tease him a lot 'cause we got
> him on the spot, welcome back.
> Welcome back, Welcome back,
> Welcome baaaaaak . . . infinity.

Riveting!

Here is an excerpt from the Chippewa Ranch Camp website. My comments are in parentheses:

> We believe that at Chippewa, each camper will find the opportunity to see her own strengths and find a greater sense of self through community living (bullshit). We realize that not every child is an athlete, or a dancer, or a horseback rider . . . and that's the true goal of Chippewa: to let every camper find her niche in a low pressure but encouraging atmosphere (bullshit).

Here is how I would write the truth as I saw it from my younger eyes:

> We believe that at Chippewa, some campers will find the opportunity to see her own lack of strength and find a greater sense of insecurity through living with a bunch of mean-spirited bullies!!!

> Man, that puberty season is a hard one! I went from being moderately popular, defined by being invited to most, not all bar mitzvahs, and some, not all, of the popular girl's boy-girl parties to being shunned, teased and slightly suicidal as evidenced by my taking three aspirin instead of two with the hopes it would end it all!

I bet you're thinking, "Wow, that's serious! Three aspirin? Poor little Shelley. Suicidal thinking at such a young age? This just can't be."

Yes, it could, and now I'll give you the backstory. So when I was in seventh grade, I was abnormally obsessed with having my period and developing, like a real life, *Are you there, God? It's me, Margaret.*

I was fascinated by the big and small breast growth of my seventh-grade peers, and could not wait to start my period and sprout some boobs. Holy Hormones! I know you are thinking

. . . oh, nevermind. I don't care what you're thinking. It's my true story of what happened, so go think what you want.

I was so fixated I started filling out a little notebook along with a friend who shall remain nameless (rhymes with Bobbin). I referred to this notebook as the People Book, and in it I drew pictures of my seventh-grade female peers with their growing buds along with a Y or N indicating whether they had begun menses, a fancy word learned during a film-strip. How I knew for sure? I have no idea.

One day we were in music class, my favorite class because as you now know, I wanted to be a singer. Sometimes we would sing in front of class. I belted out solos like, "Send In the Clowns," or, "Tomorrow," from Annie. Sometimes we would break into groups. Upon returning from a group one day, I discovered someone found the People Book. This was the beginning of the end of my moderate popularity. From then on I was teased incessantly, however, this was not yet the three-aspirin episode. It gets much worse.

Unpopular me was invited along with a popular girl to a popular boy's house. I didn't think to question why. Popular boy's parents weren't home, so it was two popular boys, a popular girl and me. Popular boys escort each of us to a different room in the unsupervised house. Being unpopular me with some daddy issues, while I didn't go all the way, I did a little more with this popular boy than was appropriate. Next thing you know, popular boy opens the blinds to reveal a bunch of kids from school standing outside laughing. It was a setup.

The next school day when I opened my locker, what seemed like hundreds of pieces of paper came spilling out with words scrawled on them including "tool," "whore" and "slut." I was thirteen.

Any afterschool special, those crises derailed my music career, that and my family moved to the city. I went to a private school lacking the infrastructure to support a true music curriculum. My school did, however, support teenage smoking by supplying a student smoking lounge. In many ways, it was a blessing. I was no longer bullied and I fit in with the rest of my schoolmates with the common denominators of sex, drugs, cigarettes and rock and roll.

Unlike public school where my mother had me tested for a learning disability because I was so traumatized that I couldn't focus, I got good grades and graduated third in my class. Subsequently, the number one kid in the class died tragically in a lawnmower accident so I guess I can say I am number two in my class.

The point of this story, and there is a point, is that I am a singer, maybe not a rock star, yet a singer of songs unsung. I sing my songs in the form of writing. I write in my own authentic voice and just as you can hear a guitar lick and identify the guitar player, my hope is that my own writing voice is uniquely identifiable.

I write because I have to write, like a singer who has to sing or a musician who has to make music. I write not so much as to have people read my writing, I write to connect, to engage, to feel less alone. I also write to allow others to feel related to what I'm writing about, to laugh, to cry, to identify within themselves similar feelings and to evoke a memory.

I used to think my journey was so unique yet it's not, and for that I am grateful.

If I can't be a rock star, then I will be a write star even if in my own eyes.

CHAPTER 31

If you think he's hot

"If you think he's hot, sleep with him and don't let him tattoo you."

Seriously. If I can share one important lesson I learned the hard way, that's it. Oh, come on, some of you have really shitty, bad tattoos. I've seen them. Some of you wish you had slept with the artist instead of living with that your whole life.

A few years back, a new tattoo studio opened in the hood. I was already sporting three mediocre tattoos at the time, however, there weren't as many great artists as there are now, and frankly, I didn't know what I didn't know.

Any hot potato, there was this hot tattoo artist at the new studio. I didn't think to sleep with him, so I decided I should let him tattoo me. Or maybe I wanted him to tattoo me and then sleep with me? I don't know. My moral compass and my taste in ink have since evolved greatly. I did look at his work in a photobook first. Swear to you.

We discussed what I wanted and then a couple days later, I go in for my appointment and Hot Guy is all ready with the gun. I get the tattoo on the right part of my upper hip, which hurt like a MOTHER! I want him to think I'm Hot Girl, and so I laugh and giggle. Haha, tee hee.

After a couple hours and, if I recall, a cigarette break or two (him, not me), the masterpiece is finished. I pulled up my pants, zipped em' and look in the mirror. What the fuck, man? That looks like CRAP, I say in my mind.

"Oh that's fantastic, wow, it looks so great, you're so hot, I want to take you home, throw you..." I say out loud to him.

Seriously, to this day when I look at my stomach I am reminded of that lesson. Now don't you forget it.

Love,

Shelley

CHAPTER 32

Intervention

Me, "It's already driving me cray-cray!"

Them, "Get out of here!"

Me, "Pleazzzzzze!"

Them, "But then you will be mad at us."

Me, "No I, I . . . okay, fine . . . I love you. Bye"

When you are a nice person, people don't mind helping you be accountable even if the absurd reality is they are losing money by helping you. Any Altruism, the good people of Supercuts have agreed to kick me out of the store whenever I walk in and want to buzz off my one-eighth-inch hair growth.

I've really enjoyed having very little hair, so frankly I am not that motivated to grow it. The only motivation is that it's a little cold. I've loved saving tons of money every month on cut, color and products and I love the ease of getting ready every day without having to deal with hair. As I type this, I am totally imagining the following scene:

Me, "It's driving me cray-cray!"

Them, "Get out of here!"

Me, "Pleazzzzzze!"

Them, "No, you will regret it!"

Me, "No, I won't!"

Them, "You made us promise."

Me, "It's okay. Really."

Them, "Get out of here, Sherry!"

Me, "It's Shelley!"

Them, "Oh, sorry. Get out of here, Shelley!"

Me, "Promises are meant to be broken!"

Them, "No. Get out!"

Who have I become? A manipulator? Someone who strongarms people and forces them to do what I want them to do? Just for today I will be a good little hair-grower and pray to stop the evil thoughts of cheating on those good people by going to Great Clips.

CHAPTER 33

iSsues

You may recall my telling you that many years ago, I walked around crying, "I want a lobotomy! I want a lobotomy!"

Mom, "You can't have a lobotomy!"

Me, "I want a lobotomy! I want a lobotomy!"

You might think I was just a crazy teenager, but you'd be wrong. I was in my thirties and still filled with the angst and drama of my nineteenth nervous breakdown.

I thought I had left all that behind until yesterday, when I wished for a soundproof room with padding where I could thrash around punching shit while screaming angry curse words and crying until my lungs wore out.

Was it because of a man? No. Was it because I need meds? Maybe, but that wasn't it. Was it because something tragic, horrifying and unacceptable happened in my life? No, it wasn't that either. Was I in my personal hell? Yes!

My personal hell is a place filled with loud, cocky, inked hipster—millennials. It's a place where every guy looks like a member of Mumford & Sons, and all the women shun make-up. No, it isn't Lollapalooza, nor an Arcade Fire concert. No, it isn't some hipster independent coffee shop serving the latest trend in cold brewed coffee and a donut. No, not a craft cocktail lounge playing Daft Punk on vinyl while everyone sits on low striped cushions and corduroy couches wearing color schemes of pants and tops that make no sense.

I'll give you a hint. A woman walked around wearing a t-shirt stating, "Data is the new bacon." Excuse me, but fuck you, it is not!

Okay, fine. Last hint. All the Mumford & Sons dudes and non-makeup wearing inked millennials are wearing the exact same shirt.

Slap yourself if you get this wrong. My hell is the APPLE STORE!

My anxiety rises the moment I walk through those glass doors, and I'm instantly overstimulated by the . . . ? By the . . . I don't know, Apple vortex? Beards? Youth? I immediately want a lobotomy!

Dark-haired dad-bod Mumford & Son carrying iPad says, "Ma'am, can you step back? There's a line here."

Middle aged me, "Yep."

Going to the Apple store is like going to the gynecologist, where you sit in an exam room wearing nothing more than a paper gown and wait for the doctor. You can't run because you have no choice.

I guess what I'm trying to say is that going to the Apple store falls somewhere between calling the cable company, the cellphone company, and/or going to the gynecologist.

Backwards baseball cap wearing woman with no make-up and dad-bod, "Can I help you, ma'am?"

Middle-aged anxiety-riddled me in a low kind of growl, "I have an appointment with a genius."

Dad-bod woman, "Great. Go sit at that table with all the other pissed people, and someone will be with you in a thousand hours."

A thousand hours later . . .

Me, "My computer is not working right. Safari beeps and then the system just freezes."

Slouchy dad-bod, bearded Arcade Fire dude, "Okay, I will run some diagnostics to check the blah, blah, blah blah. It will take a hundred hours. You can just sit here and wait on the ultra-modern, totally uncomfortable stool where your feet can simply dangle while you watch all the young people text. Be right back."

Middle-aged me, feet dangling, "Okay."

Slouchy dad-bod dude comes back a hundred hours later. "We tried all the diagnostics and now need you to back up your computer with this ninety-dollar external hard drive, because you bought into the whole store-it-in-the-cloud Carbonite bullshit. So, now you need to back up your data which, by the way, is the new bacon, bring your computer back tomorrow and we will reinstall the operating system but first you need to make another Genius appointment. The first available slot is at a million o'clock."

I have a suggestion to elevate the obligatory Apple store visit. iTinis! iTinis for everyone.

iTinis can make you less iRrate, less iRational and less iRritated. Unless you have an iSsue. If you have an iSsue, you can't have an iTini, though iTinis can make you less iRrate, less iRational and less iRritated.

Really folks, I would buy the first round using Apple Pay!

CHAPTER 34

Istress

I tend to be on top of things such as dental appointments, paying bills, my dog's vaccinations, and taxes, not to mention I never run out of anything. No, really. I don't.

Back in February, after receiving my tax returns, the topic of taxes came up with some accountant friends who suggested I use TurboTax. Now, most people don't like to do taxes, in fact some people actually dread it. I get the many reasons why, however my taxes are very uncomplicated. I don't have any dependents, no 1099s, no additional interest income, just income from a job, so pretty straightforward.

As someone who sells software, I would rate my user experience with TurboTax a five out of five. The UI, user interface, is kind of cool and modern, the user experience is as fun and easy as doing taxes online can be. The site almost cheers you along as you input the necessary information. I ended up feeling like it took minimal effort to complete the process of filing both my federal and state taxes, and I didn't even mind paying. Okay, maybe a little, because I come from a fragile people. They make tracking your return very easy and I was given a range of when to expect my money . . . *until* . . .

One day I opened up the mailbox, usually just to take whatever is in there and throw it out in order to make more room for more stuff I'm just going to throw out. I pay all my bills online so any mail I receive is basically junk with the exception of my local grocery coupon. Any USPS, I went to the mailbox to purge its contents until I saw it . . . a letter from the IRS. I'm like, *what now?*

Last year I did my taxes wrong because I was on Cobra for a month. I screwed up my taxes and ended up owing. Any health care information, I take the letter out of the box and open it up. The letter informs me to call a certain number and make an appointment at a TAC, Taxpayer Assistance Center, to verify my identity.

I asked my accountant friend about it and he said to call them. I called the number and asked why I was being asked to do this. I was told there is quite a bit of identity theft going on and there is no way to get around going in person to the TAC.

We schedule the appointment for April 21, more than a month after my expected return date. Not so happy with the cute UI, user experience and payment to TurboTax, as part of the fee is to receive your return quicker.

I ended up getting an earlier appointment when I called to change the first one on April 21. I will be traveling for work and expected them to say, "Okay, we can schedule you for November." But much to my surprise, when I asked if they had something on April 5, they said yes. I was very happy with the kind IRS lady and after a round of God bless yous, and her explaining to me that I should not be late and to get there fifteen minutes early as they are very structured with regards to the times, we hung up.

One of my friends and I joked around about my ID. I have a wig on in my driver's license photo, I'm a brunette in my passport photo, and currently my hair is slightly lavender. She suggested I bring my wig which, now that I think of it, may have added levity to the day.

I get a file folder out, write TAXES with a sharpie, and fill the folder with all the required documents and ready all my various IDs.

Fast forward to today. I took the day off. It's raining like crazy. River and I have taken two walks already to try to get him to poop, we've come home totally drenched. I am already feeling cheated out of my day off, not to mention that due to the rain, I am home and they are drilling and hammering right above my head in the condo upstairs.

My appointment is at 9:30 a.m. I request an Uber at 8:55 a.m. Fifteen dollars! *What?* To go a mile and a half?! Oh, well. I get in the Uber and traffic is a disaster because of the rain. I'm already feeling shitty because I've been soaked twice and now I'm running late for an appointment for which I was told to be early. Okay, nothing I can do.

I get to the Taxpayer Assistance Center and check in at the desk. I apologize for being late and the nice lady says, "It's okay, we have a ten-minute grace period."

The waiting room is empty with the exception of two young women. I look at the sign:
- No Eating, No Drinking.
- No Weapons.
- No Cell Phone Conversations.

I know there was another NO but I can't remember. Any short-term memory loss, one of the women kept coughing and coughing, nonstop coughing while the other woman loudly explained how her IUD fell out which, long story short, is the reason she unexpectedly has a second child.

I am now waiting over thirty minutes. Two more people come in. This time it's a young woman with an elderly woman appearing to have no teeth. After a few minutes, I hear the younger woman talking about the wait. I tell them I have been here for thirty minutes. The younger woman explains to me that they are here to verify her mother's identity, the one with no teeth. I explain that's the same reason I'm here.

After forty-eight minutes and a bladder full of coffee, they call my number and I am told to go to room ten. Room ten isn't really a room, more like a desk with a door in front of it. I am greeted with a non-smiling, "Hello, how are you?"

Instead of spreading sunshine, I explain, "I should have brought a book today and not had any fluids."

She gives me a blank look and asks for my ID and then for my tax forms. I hand her my wig-wearing license and take out my nice little folder with all my information and *holy hellish horrific realization,* my tax form is not there. I have my lease, my passport with the brown hair photo, my social security card, my 2015 tax returns, my 2016 W2s, but no tax return.

I put my hand to my forehead, shake my head and tears start welling up.

I tell her, "Just give me a moment, please."

I sift through the papers in my folder a little slower and state unemotionally, "I'm going to stab myself in the eye."

The lady asks, "Did you file online?"

I say, "Yes."

She says, "Try to look up your return on your phone."

I am trying to look at my shitty small phone with watery eyes (and without readers), and again state very matter-of-factly, "I'm going to stab myself in the eye."

She says, "I'll be right back."

Somehow I am able to reset my TurboTax password and access the return. A moment later, another woman enters the room and states, "I am a commissioner with the IRS and you made a statement that has us concerned, and we take these things very seriously."

Holy 1040 form! The IRS really does care!

I smile and say, "Fuck you, I was only kidding!"

No really, I said, "Oh my gosh. That was just an expression. Thank you for your concern."

"Stab myself in the eye," comes from some SNL skit a long time ago. Maybe I should retire it, like the word "neat," which I mistakenly used with a millennial in my workplace who happens to be my director who has agreed to never tell anyone I actually used that word to describe another human being.

So I finally make it out of the IRS office, walk River, get drenched and instead of stabbing myself in the eye by rolling up the 2016 tax return I forgot to add into my nice little folder, I sit down to write this story with the drilling and hammering overhead. Soon it will be time to walk River again but luckily, my tax return should be back in nine weeks, "If not, please call this number."

If you are ever called to the TAC, I would like to add the following to list of NOs:

- No drinking before you arrive at the TAC (if you have to pee, you will miss your turn).
- No worrying about being late, they have a ten-minute grace period.
- No audible statement of doing bodily harm to oneself.

Check that you have your forms, your ID and your IUD.

Love,

Shelley

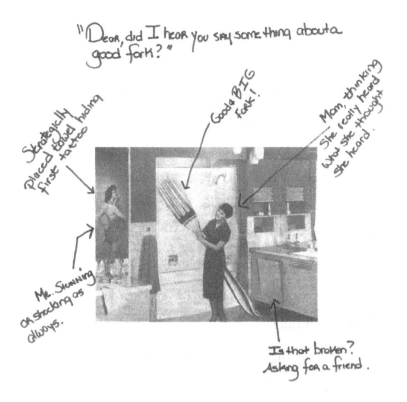

"Dear, did I hear you say something about a good fork?"

Goods BIG fork!

Mom, thinking she really heard what she thought she heard.

Strategically placed towel hiding first tattoo

Me. Stunning or stocking as always.

Is that broken? Asking for a friend.

CHAPTER 35

It's interesting being bald

Some interesting things have happened since shaving my head. People have been commenting that I have a nice head. Who knew? You really wouldn't know unless you shaved it.

I find myself noticing other people's shaved heads. It's kind of like gaydar for bald people—baldar. My baldar became finely tuned quickly. It leads me to notice what's going on with other people's heads. Do they have rolls of skin above their neck? Do they have indents or zits? Scabs or scars?

This morning, I was in my building elevator with a bald guy. He complimented my head, "I like your head. You have really a nice head."

We had never spoken before. I looked at his head and noticed it was really nice, too. We shared a moment only two hairless people can share. We stood there and admired each other's head until the elevator reached the ground floor and we went ahead with our day.

I was bored in the shower this morning because now there is less to do, so I conditioned my nonhair head to make it smell good like my hair did. I don't want people to just tell me I have a nice head. I want people to tell me my head smells like sunshine or flowers. Like sometimes when you smell your dog because they smell like your puppy but please, I don't want to smell like a puppy.

Any hair follicle, I am excited because when I tell people I am totally wigging out, I will mean it. I'm going to the wig store and am super excited! I'm sure I'll have great stories from that experience. By the way, Eminem didn't wear a hoodie because he wanted to look like a gangsta. It's frickin' cold when you don't have hair.

Wanna hair something funny? I have a flat iron! Guys, that's the opposite of a curling iron, it's used to straighten hair. It's been years since my hair was long enough to use one. Guess the flat iron is in good company with the pantyhose.

Holy Hot Rollers! This has been an amazing experience so far. I threw out some half-used hair products today, and laughed and laughed. What the follicle, right? I may keep my head this way for a bit, or maybe grow it just a hair.

CHAPTER 36

Let love rule

A wise man by the name of Lenny Kravitz once said, "You've got to let love rule," and being the rule follower that I am, I follow his rule.

You see, from the time I can remember, I've always loved love. In fact, I would say that I am a creator of love. No, this isn't my version of *The Secret*. I mean like starting with Barbie and Ken, love always prevailed no matter the scenario my little girl fantasy mind conjured up, including:

- War, as in Ken returning from war, often without a limb (I was a young girl during the seventies, Viet Nam).
- Temptation, in the form of another woman, Skipper.
- Poverty in the form of only having a Kleenex box for a bed.
- Vanity in the form of a failed beauty shop visit at the hands of my eight-year-old cosmetology skills.

Love always prevails.

I was thinking about love throughout the decades of my life. In the 1960s, we were told to smile on each other and love one another right now.

In the 1970s, we were told that love would keep us together.

In the 1980s, love was, well . . . endless.

In the 1990s, things continued to stay on the up and up because you loved me (strangely past tense, but what ev).

In the early 2000s, we even found love in a hopeless place.

In 2019, LinkedIn introduced additional reactions including the heart indicating "love to express deep resonance and support."

As a corporate mindfulness facilitator, I invite people to explore the practice of mindfulness not only to help cultivate a greater sense of wellbeing including stress reduction, focus and resilience, I also help people learn to use the practice as a foundation for self-awareness which involves mindfulness of body sensations, feeling tones, and thoughts and the way our minds construct meaning to really see how we are being in real time.

Let's use my friend Carol Campos as an example. Carol is a life coach who incorporates storytelling and metaphor with her messages about various subjects, including finding our purpose, place and our unique gifts. Let's say Carol posts something on LinkedIn, I read it and choose to practice self-awareness:

1. I sense my physical sensation. Upon reading Carol's post, I feel energy in the area of my heart, and I smile.
2. I sense the feeling tone is pleasant. There are only three feeling tones—pleasant, unpleasant and neutral.
3. I observe my thoughts and think, "This is very interesting and I understand how this pertains to my life."
4. I get in touch with what the thoughts means, "I love this."

What usually happens next is I comment and click on the heart reaction.

So here's a question, how do you decide when to use the "like" reaction and when to use the "love" reaction? Do you actually think about it? Are you hesitant to use it?

I ask this question because I believe that many of us withhold love in the context of work or anything business related, and yet in the next instant, we find ourselves eating a cookie or drinking a glass of wine, and unabashedly expressing, "OMG! I love this."

As noted earlier, I've always loved love, and when I reflect of the best mentors I ever had in life, they include two former managers, Linda McNairy and Dan Marks. I think of them not only with tremendous respect, but also LOVE (I love you, Dan and Linda, if you are reading this). The best companies I ever worked for were the places where people love each other.

Can you imagine what it would be like if we were really able to sense into the love that we feel and actually express it? Can you imagine how expansive, inclusive, connecting, nurturing, compassionate, empowering, and inviting it would be?

We hear about so many who feel disconnected, marginalized, and stressed at work. What would it feel like to show a little love?

I would like to express my *love* for you, for your content that expands my heart, makes it smile, sing, sometimes cry...

A wise man, Lenny Kravitz once said,

> Love transcends all space and time
> And love can make a little child smile
> Oh can't you see
> This won't go wrong
> But we got to be strong
> We can't do it alone
>
> We got to let love rule

CHAPTER 37

Let's dance

I handed him my credit card with one hand while wiping away tears hidden by my sunglasses. It's one thing to cry in the Naturalizer store when buying the same pair of shoes the salesclerk said her grandma just bought (I took those back), but this was Nordstrom! *Not in my store* where shoes jump out at you like technicolor dreams, where rows of cosmetics are like the yummy candy-filled scene in *Willy Wonka,* and dresses flitter and dance like colorful confetti thrown in celebration. How is it possible that I would be crying in Nordstrom?

The poor sales guy would show me a pair of shoes and I would recoil as if I had just seen some deformed parasitic twin coming from a man's stomach, "Horrible."

"Don't even pick that one up."

"Is that a real color?"

Oh, and those shameful designers at Cole Haan should just punch themselves in the eye. The dear man, with a knowing look, totally empathized with me as he brought out shoe after shoe. He even went for Fendi and Ferragamo. Even those were horrible, and they cost more than a new couch.

Fine! My YSL's are rotting in the closet until I can make some great Parisian-inspired art piece, or maybe I can wear them while I am horizontal when that special someone comes over.

In the meantime, this comfort shoe thing is a travesty. I don't want to offend anyone, and I know there are people with no shoes at all, and I obviously realize there are some with no feet for that matter, and some with bunions that can't fit into regular shoes without experiencing great pain. I am sorry.

Truly, I am.

I can't bear to wear flats, and it's not a height thing. The rounded toe of the ballet slipper-style shoes do not appeal to me. Let's face it, none of us over thirty, forty, fifty and on, are ballerinas. No, girls, pilates is not ballet.

I've been told I am built like a ballerina but I've also been told I dance like a stripper. Did you ever ask someone how they thought you dance? You may be in shock, or maybe they will be.

I ended up buying a pair of comfort shoes to get me through the airport part of my travels, however I ended up wearing flip-flops and was able to wear a small heel for the conference.

Yesterday afternoon, I flip-flopped over to Nordstrom, returned the comfort shoes, said hello to a pair of peacock-blue Jimmy Choo shoes (I didn't buy them), and flip-flopped out of the store with one hundred fifty dollars back in my back account.

Let's dance!

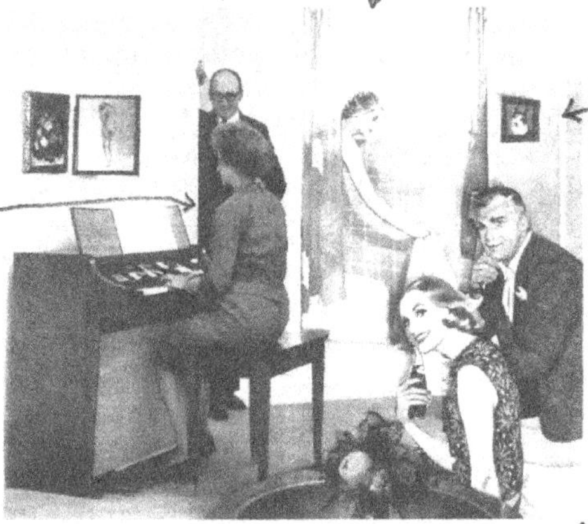

CHAPTER 38

Liver

Why? Why?

I ran screaming out of the house to get away from it. She did it again. Was it to punish me? I can still conjure it up in my mind's nose, the smell of liver on the stove.

Holy posttraumatic smell disorder! I have flashbacks of that smell, a mixture of sweet, putrid, funk. She hardly ever cooked anything so why did she have to cook liver when the smell made me cry? Apparently, I come from an organ eating people, however I choose to not carry on this tradition

Any icky, it's remarkable to me how we can conjure up smells in our mind no matter how many years have gone by, like the greasy grilled cheese and tomato soup day in the school cafeteria. I wonder if they used lard back then?

I can smell my grandmother's house in my mind. I thought it was an old house smell, but it's just now that I am writing this and after all these years I realize the predominant smell of that house was the oil paint she used to paint and teach art in her basement mixed with her Raleigh cigarettes.

A memory will trigger an instant smell such as tequila. Can you smell it right now? I can, and now I want to recall the smell of Tide Pods!

Any emanation, I don't understand why people can't smell themselves. I was in a cycling class and could barely breathe due to the stink of the guy next to me. How often do you get in an elevator overwhelmed by an unfriendly perfume or someone gives you a big friendly hug and they end up unknowingly fragrancing it forward? Taxi anyone? Patchouli? Dead fish on beach?

I love memories and I love how they can trigger smells in my mind, or vice versa. I hope I don't smell in spin class.

The smell of coffee is one of my favorites. I love that I can recall the smell my mom's perfume, the way my dogs smelled, the smell of sex, the smell of art museums and books…

I hope you are having good memories right now.

Love,

Shelley

CHAPTER 39

Lovely

"Your life depends on it?"

"But I can't do it. I'm trying as hard as I can!"

"You have to try, Shelley. Your life depends on it!"

"There is just no way I can do this!"

I'm given the life or death challenge of having to read something so small without my readers. I simply can't do it and that's how it ends and I die.

Why is it I can't read the name of the color on the bottom of a bottle of nail polish and yet I can clearly see every nuance and new wrinkle of my face? Not complaining, just noticing so you don't have to give me compliments or tell me to embrace aging. I would simply rather laugh at it and, oh yes, get Botox.

Okay stop you haters. My body, my choice!

I do believe my true calling would have been to be the official color namer for an internationally known nail polish brand. I mean, I do it all the time.

"Shelley, I love that nail color. What is it?"

Are you fucking kidding me? I say in my head but what comes out my mouth is, "Purple Passion Prostitute," or "Road Rage Red."

There was a time not that long ago where I could actually read the "Peel Here" words on the label of the bottom of the polish.

I was thinking about the different eyewear that would be useful in life, such as frosted glasses with which to look at ones aging self in a kinder and gentler way, or rose-colored glasses to soothe and ease the reality of life. Maybe x-ray glasses to see inside the mind of my partner since I usually have no idea what he is really thinking.

"It's been lovely, Pru. Just lovely," he says when he is leaving me for good.

"Ummm, okay." Somehow, I'm not surprised and that's how it ends.

My partner is British and emotionally reserved. I, on the other hand, on an emotional scale from one to ten am... oh, never mind, why put a measurement on it?

Any over the top, typical conversations go like this:

Me, "How was your day?"

Him, "Lovely. Just lovely."

Me the second time, "How was your day?"

Him the second time, "It was just lovely."

Me the third time, "How was your day?"

Him, "Just peachy!"

So you may be surprised how I die because I can't read small fonts, but maybe you won't be so surprised by the cluelessly abandoned:

You ask, "Shelley, how could you not know this was coming? Weren't there any signs?"

Me, "Nope."

You in a more insistent voice, "That's impossible. You had to have known."

Me, "Nope."

You softening your tone, "Are you okay?"

Me, "Lovely. I tell you. Just lovely."

I know you are thinking "Pru?" What's this "Pru" thing? Well, I will tell you except I really honestly can't remember how it happened, however, suffice it to say my pet name is Prudence and therefore my shortened pet name is Pru.

I like this nickname except while I am writing this, I am thinking it reminds of me of the word "prune" and now this story is coming full circle, wrinkles on my face, Botox . . . stop haters! My body, my choice. Frosted glasses STAT!

It's interesting to be at this point in life. I am not old and I am not young, I'm middle. For a period of time, transitioning to middle was really difficult. I noticed every little change. I felt unprepared and pissed off that Judy Blume never wrote the sequel to *Are you there, God? It's me, Margaret.*

Just as naming nail polish colors is my true calling, I could have written a really great title for that sequel. Instead, I will just live it out by being middle, "Just lovely," maybe or maybe not getting Botox, hopefully not abandoned, never caring about the name of the color of my nail polish and noticing changes without judgment nor frosted glasses.

Namaste.

CHAPTER 40

Magic door

If I slept until 6:30 a.m. or later, I would think I died. I would open my eyes, look at the clock in disbelief and think, Holy small space! Why does heaven look exactly the same as my shitty tiny dorm room apartment, and why is my dog Potato here? Did he die too? I would be completely disoriented and in a state of shock and bewilderment. That is only if I wasn't sick. If I was sick, it would all make sense and I would think, "Oh, I get it now. I'm sick."

I would probably get a call from my mom at some point in the morning and if her Momdar detected any illness in my vocal quality, she would immediately tell me to, "Go get a throat culture! You always get Strep throat," even though it's been thirty years since I've had Strep.

Any hallucinogenics, this weird girl has never been able to sleep late. I would sit on the family room floor, too close to the TV, which is probably why I had to start wearing glasses in third grade, watch cartoons, eat Quisp Cereal or Captain Crunch and occasionally whimper like a lonely, motherless puppy. The other Browns slept in while I entertained myself by cutting the roof of my mouth shoveling in shards of hard sugary cereal. I still kind of like burning the roof of my mouth with really hot coffee. It makes little blisters that I can play with using my tongue. If the weird fits...

I once went to the doctor with a mouth full of blisters in a total freak-out panic, oh shit, my life is over, what the hell is wrong with me and who did this to me, only to discover the cause was acid from too much balsamic vinegar. Kind of like the time I mistook bruises for ringworm.

There weren't any talk shows on TV on the weekends, so I have no idea what I watched. The Magic Door, a local show, was on. The nerdy, tights-clad host from the Magic Door actually married me. No, no, I didn't marry the Magic Door guy. He performed my marriage ceremony without tights.

On the show, he came out of a magic door, and the door was from an acorn. Maybe he was the inspiration for my very favorite Sponge Bob Square Pants, "Who lives in a Pineapple under the Sea?" Some of you call "drugs" on that one. I call PURE GENIUS shouting in my very best Oprah imitation.

Can you hear it? Essentially, I was married by a man from an acorn. You?

Speaking of marriage, my former husband can confirm this. Every night we would watch some show that started at 9 p.m. and, like clockwork, I would pass out at 9:50 p.m., never seeing the end to any program. He would have to recount to me what happened the next day. I wonder if he ever made up an ending.

Any tree hugger, It's hard to be in the minority with the early morning thing. I prefer not to stay up late because I wake up too early and can't fall back asleep. "So what?" You say?

What is that without at least six hours of sleep, I basically function like your friend's five year-old. The one who you have to continuously tell your friend what a beautiful, wonderful, remarkable, God's giftable this child is when he is splayed out on the floor, bawling with the high-pitched, ear-piercing scream of a wounded animal because he needs a nap. That's kind of how I get. Just switch the adjectives "high-pitched, ear-piercing" with something that includes tears, cursing about how screwed up everything is and how much my life sucks. Any dateless, for a good time, call me at 7 a.m.

The impetus for this story happened last night. When at 7:30 p.m., I changed into pajamas and washed off my makeup after having dressed and put on makeup just thirty minutes prior, determined to go out even just for one drink. I then declined two invitations for plans commencing after 8:30 p.m., picked up carry-out, put in a DVD, fell asleep before it ended, and returned it this morning. If I run into my ex, I will ask him about the ending.

Have a happy day.

Love,

Shelley

CHAPTER 41

Megabus

Bleeding or leakage? Either way it was almost unbearable. Here I am stuffed into a crowded, small space on the megabus with all of my closest new friends, and I mean closest. The only thing mega about the bus was its size, allowing for as many people as possible to be crammed in to go somewhere cheap.

You know how sometimes on a crowded train one of your body parts is touching someone else's? You really have no choice in the matter, and you would never dare get this close to a total stranger if it were your decision, even if it were a game of Truth or Dare you might choose truth as opposed to the "I dare you to stand so close to *that* person and you must feel his sweaty shoulder touching yours."

You know the world is a strange place when imaginary protocol dictates you stand at least eight feet from that person at an ATM.

Well, the megabus is more like the train except you can't get off. No, it will be hours before you get off.

It's hot and I just know there are lice somewhere on this bus and I'm certain to smell like the ashtray of the man behind me oozing from his breath and body right into my lack of hair.

I'm surrounded by at least five people wearing headphones, and all I can hear is the bass thumping and pounding from the bleeding or leakage. I put my headphones on and listen to the soothing sounds of Burt Bacharach, I mean Led Zeppelin. Holy Houses of the Holy, I can't get my music loud enough to cover up the bleeding and leakage.

I knew this was going to be an interesting experience when the megabus pulled up and one of the first passengers exiting was a thousand year-old man with a big, angry, purple-reddish contusion on his forehead. I think he may have taken a tumble off a megabus recently, leaving some DNA samples in his trail and certainly whatever seat he occupied during his most recent ride.

"Sir, I am going to recline my chair just a bit," I say politely to the man scrunched behind me to avoid any sort of physical damage. In a raised voice he states, "I am really uncomfortable here and..."

I raise my voice stating, "So am I!"

I turn around and immediately feel bad and yet struggling with the fact that I too paid for this shitty bus ride. I pull the lever and recline about a quarter inch.

Take that, Mr. Icky Man!

I am now an angry, hot, cramped megabus rider with betrayed personal boundaries who now smells, probably has lice and bloody DNA on me. Where are the Naugahyde seats of yesteryear? Where are the runaways? Where is the weird?

Finally, we are back in Chicago. I apologize to the man behind me and he apologizes back.

I go home and wash that bus right out of lack of hair and body...

Dorm sweet dorm.

"The sick day"

OK, fine! Mental Health DAY! We know em'! We love em'!

Look! Total brow envy ✖

Yeah, No! Can't do my own nails.

Life is better with Pugs of any dog(s)

↑ Do you remember to put on your favorite music to help you get the good feels?

CHAPTER 42

Member of the tribe

This story is a celebration of how interconnected we are as human beings, something that has become increasingly apparent during this season in our lives.

I love traveling, airport bars, airplane stories, and people watching at airports, just not flight delays. Several years ago on a flight to D.C., I chose to sit in the very last row when paying my ridiculous change fee to an airline, which shall remain unnamed but starts with an A.

I chose to sit in the last row because I like to be close to the lavatory (one of those strange words most of us use in only one situation). I have this thing about the fear of being far away from it, stuck in a middle seat, navigating the beverage cart, or worse yet, having a window seat in the middle of the plane and making everyone get up more than once during an hour and half flight, so I chose the last row.

I was hoping no one would sit next to me, as if giving the stink-eye would prevent someone from actually daring to sit next to this menacing, five-foot-one, buck-five woman.

Then he came. I heard the cough and was like, *oh, crap, a smoker.* The smoker stood at my row to nonverbally communicate for me to get my ass up. Then, right behind him, *she* followed.

He took the window seat and she took the middle. They looked Hispanic and also looked like bikers, as in motorcycle. I like bikers, they are typically a friendly people. This I know from my time dating a Harley tour guide who took me across the country on Route 66 with a group of twenty-five international Hog riders. Thankfully, I did not detect a hint of stale cigarette smoke emanating from her.

As we untangled our seatbelts, I had one part of hers and she mine, the conversation began.

"I hope you won't mind the smell of turkey and peanut butter," I said. "I brought it for lunch."

"No, I don't mind, we just had McDonald's," she replied.

I don't eat McDonald's but could tell by her dialect she was from another part of the country. She pronounced "Mac" like "Mack," while most people in Chicago pronounce the "Mac" part like "Mick" as in Jagger.

"What are you going to do in D.C.?"

For some reason I felt compelled to keep the conversation going. I for sure thought she was going to respond with the usual touristy thing.

"We are meeting with the USDA," she said.

"Are you a meat inspector?" I asked recalling my late father who was a meat inspector in the army. A little ironic to me, given he was in veterinary school at the time.

"No, I am meeting with the USDA to get more food for my tribe." *What?* This was no Hispanic biker!

"Your tribe?" I said with complete fascination.

So this is how one of the most interesting conversations I have ever had in my life began. Roxanne is the chairman of the Crow Creek Sioux Tribe from South Dakota. Seriously, I can count on less than one hand how many people I have ever met from South Dakota, and aside from bikers visiting Sturgis, I have never met anyone who has been to South Dakota that I know of, and now I was sitting next to a Native American Indian. I felt privileged, honored and fascinated.

I began gingerly asking her questions while checking with her that it was okay to ask. We talked about everything from Bernie Sanders, alcoholism and the terrible meth problem with the youth of the reservation. We talked about spirituality, the sweat lodge built behind her home, the heated rocks and prayer circle where Roxanne could see spirits and eagles.

We spoke of buffalos, celebrational pow wows, poverty, casinos, land ownership, and how the young people from her tribe meet others to marry without marrying into their own tribe to avoid marrying a relative.

We talked about smudging sage and tobacco for healing, and how she often spreads these sacred items around her home counterclockwise as she prays. Together we Googled her tribe and looked at images. She would point to someone and tell me a story or that they were probably an auntie.

Just before I began to eat my lunch, Roxanne adopted me into the tribe. She said, "We make this official by eating."

Now a Crow Creek Dakota Indian adoptee, I happily ate my turkey and peanut butter on my gluten-free bread.

Roxanne was so gracious and forthcoming. I must have asked her a hundred questions while she held a small red cloth roll of sacred tobacco in her hand during the entire flight. At one point, her ears began to hurt terribly and as I rubbed her back, she rubbed her pouch of healing tobacco around her face and ears.

When we landed, she thanked me for being so interested and for my desire to learn about her culture. We both agreed it wasn't about our backgrounds, we were two women who bonded on a spiritual level.

As we said our goodbyes, we hugged each other long and hard. I have her address and plan on keeping in touch. I hope to have the opportunity to visit my new friend, especially now that I am an adopted member of the tribe.

I have had time to think about this extraordinary meeting. If we would just be open and take the time to learn about the people who are different from us . . . well, you know . . . I don't want to end the story with a cliché.

Ask, learn, love, appreciate differences, find similarities.

This story is dedicated to Roxanne and my new tribe, the Crow Creek Sioux Tribe of Fort Thompson, South Dakota.

We are all connected.

"Your Friends & Family"

I mean, this weirdness is everything!

Elephant in the room...

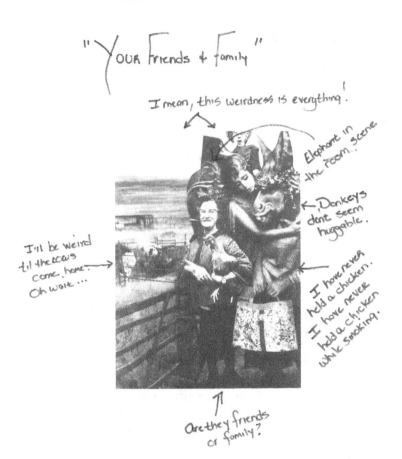

← Donkeys dont seem huggable.

I'll be weird til the cows come home. Oh wait...

I have never held a chicken. I have never held a chicken while smoking.

Are they friends or family?

CHAPTER 43

Mice

My dog and I just stared at the mouse. The mouse stared back at us. We all stood there frozen. I went to the kitchen and saw it right in the middle of the floor. He just stopped and stared at me. I called for my Pug, thinking there was something he could do, but as soon as he ran toward the sound of my voice and saw the mouse, he froze, too.

In the early days when I was married, we lived in this very old walk-up on Scott Street. It was a beautiful place. The entire apartment had maple floors except for the maid's quarters. Apparently, back in the day the poor maid had a separate entrance and her tiny little room had oak floors. That should put her in her place!

Lee Miglin previously owned the building. Remember Andrew Cunanon, the guy who killed Versace? He also killed Lee Miglin in the house across the street from ours.

By the way, Lee Miglin's wife, Marilyn, was a very famous Chicagoan, and a world-famous speaker and author in the beauty industry. She married after Lee's death and that guy dropped dead during plastic surgery.

Talk about weird, someone apparently died on the same block while trying to bring a bottle of wine to the chick he was banging by jumping from a balcony to the balcony below and became impaled on the wrought iron railing. Stairs? Not so much...

One day I was sitting in my home office and saw these kids running across my fire escape right out my window. I was like WTF? Turns out the neighbor who lived in this huge ten-million-dollar mansion had a child porn and drug thing going on and the FBI had raided his house.

The street couldn't be any weirder.

So back to the mice problem. Well now after writing this, it just doesn't seem as big a deal after impalement, murder, child porn and oak floors.

Have a nice day.

Love,

Shelley

CHAPTER 44

Middle age

I am either having a midlife crisis or just one of my usual nervous breakdowns, or maybe both. It's been really ugly. I've been really ugly.

The usual nervous breakdown part started with the holidays but the middle-aged crisis started because of Madonna. In my younger days, Madonna set the bar for me. She was a sexy, fit, badass! I never cared much for her music but loved everything about her. In my eyes, she was the kind of woman who could strike a pose and give guys an immediate boner.

Any hard times, in my younger days, it was instilled in the core of my being that looks were everything and that you could never be too thin and blah, blah barf. Yeah, sometimes...

Any oversharing and parental issues, Madonna set the bar for me. I actually met her when I was a concierge. She was a guest at the hotel where I worked for a few months while on location filming. She was a badass, she acted like a badass, and she was beautiful. Her chiseled body was ridiculous! I was in awe and inadequate. I would smoke my Marlboros, starve and cry over Madonna longing to be like the Material Girl. She exuded confidence and a "I don't have to tell you not to fuck with me, I DARE you to!"

Several years later, the Marlboros were gone and I had become a new iteration, a different physical version of myself. I was now a marathoner, a spin instructor, and a more chiseled athletic woman. Still defining myself by my body as a measurement of my self-esteem, I felt powerful, confident (aka false ego), sexy, and had the "I know you probably want to get some of this but you can't fuck with me," attitude. I rolled like this for a number of years until *that* thing happened.

That thing was a series of events in a very dark and terrifying season of my life. The blessing in it was I had to find a new way to define myself, and ultimately I learned I am just who I am, and not what my body looks like or my chronological age.

Any un-ultimately and unlearning, Madonna is again defining how I feel about myself. How is it possible Madonna is now looking old to me? How is it possible she is less than a handful of years older than me? How is it possible the woman who could slay men and women with her dominatrix-like power, oozing vexing sensuality mixed with danger, doesn't look sexy to me anymore? Why is it that I would no longer want to make out with Madonna?

Why? Because I am, yet again, letting my outsides define who I am. Not only am I doing it to myself, I am doing it to other women around my age. Looking at others and myself through the lens of our society that makes it really hard for a woman to not only be okay with aging, but to be okay at any age.

My dear friends, I needed to come clean about something I am doing that is so destructive, self-damaging, derogatory and ugly. I can now clearly see the elephant in the room is *me*.

Elephants don't belong in rooms, and damaging thoughts don't belong in our hearts.

I am going to kick the elephant out of the room, slay this shit, and embrace the most important truth I've ever learned.

> I am not what I do or what I
> look like. I am just who I am.

I don't judge you that way. I am going to give myself, others and Madonna a break for being beautiful female human beings who can't help but get older. There is no more room for the elephant, there is only room for an abundance of:

Compassion,

Gentleness,

Kindness,

Gratitude,

and above all else, LOVE.

I am so much more. I have so much more. Sometimes I forget and I'm sorry.

I love you.

CHAPTER 45

Mile high

"Thirty-eight years, and she's been at it for forty-four!"

Holy holding pattern! Two flight attendants with a combined experience of eighty-two years, and this was just in coach. Maybe if I had asked the other two flight attendants in first class, I bet it would be close to two hundred years of combined flight experience. That's a lot of cockpit and pantyhose!

Any height and weight requirement, I was imagining these stewardesses years ago in their twenties, single, meeting weight requirements, looking just a touch below Hollywood standards like real living Barbie dolls with excitement in their eyes, fending off ass grabbers and horny Ken-doll-looking pilots. I was in love with any unrealistic and unachievable female standard, which is why as young girl I wanted to grow up to be five-foot-nine dressed like Cher in Bob Mackie, a stewardess or a playboy bunny.

Any mile high club, I wondered how many times each of these ladies uttered, "Federal law prohibits tampering with, disabling, or destroying a lavatory smoke detector."

Why is an airplane bathroom called a lavatory? The origin of the word comes from late Middle English: from Latin lavatorium "place for washing," from Latin lavare "to wash." The word originally denoted something in which to wash, such as a bath. No one really washes themselves in an airplane lavatory. They do other things, for example smoke or have sex.

I smoked on an airplane many times. Yes, this weird girl used to smoke. Can you believe it? I can't! When I was in college, they still had the smoking section on airplanes. Holy disgustingness!

On my flight home from L.A., I was all geared up with my headphones in eager anticipation of the inflight movie. This time I didn't have adulterers sitting next to me like I did on the way out of ORD, just two young guys discussing the benefits of creatine supplements. One was wearing Bulls shorts. Some of you know I have a hard and fast rule about flying, and that is to dress nice, which was the proper standard for flying about thirty years ago. Even when I smoked on the plane, I was quite stunning in whatever flight appropriate apparel I was wearing. For some reason, I still follow this nonsensical rule.

The movie starts and within seconds the flight attendant announces, "We apologize, however we are having technical issues and the audio portion is only in Spanish."

The movie was turned off. A few seconds later the movie started again, in Spanish, "We apologize, however there will be no movie."

Ay Carumba!

Not five minutes later, a flight attendant a few rows up, no longer a perky, young stewardess and maybe not even well-manicured, who would know with the latex gloves they wear to throw your crap into the garbage bag they carry through the aisles, I hear her say "No habla Espinol," in response to a passenger. I felt sorry for this man. He would have liked the movie.

Fly the friendly skies but not in Spanish.

" Cheers Chicago "

You can take the girl out of Chicago but you can't take Chicago out of the girl.

So many miles + hours on this lakefront path.

Me toasting my Sweet Home CHICAGO

Gibson's Martinis Best in town

Chicago Steakhouses

CHAPTER 46

Minivan

"No, we are not there yet! Don't make me stop this car…"

"I am not staying in Minnesota!"

I sat at a table outside the meeting room feverishly trying to find a flight. I would go to a travel site, find an available seat, frantically type in my credit card to book it, and immediately the flight would become unavailable.

Someone had literally started a fire that shut down all the Chicago airports! I was almost in tears. Desperation filled my entire being. Such an utter feeling of fear, helplessness and vulnerability! Fuck it! I am going to slay this frickin' situation like the badass I am.

Okay, not really. It was more like I don't have clean panties, I'm afraid of the Mall of America because it's like Vegas without as many drunks and whores, and I am gonna get home no matter what I have to do! So I called Enterprise, the company that "picks you up!"

Holy hurry up! This was personal! This was my weekend! No offense to anyone in Minnesota, but I felt like a caged animal in this Dumpletree Hotel for the last two nights. I had a karaoke date to get to tonight!

Enterprise came to the rescue after I called them three times to ask, "Are you sure you have a car for me? Do you promise?"

"Yes!" for the third time.

The nice shuttle driver girl took me to the local branch. The ten-minute ride felt like an hour. Any impatience, I filled out the paperwork and got upgraded to a minivan. Laugh if you will, but this bitch had lumbar support and Sirius XM! Holy octane and lithium, LET'S GO!

Watch your fluid intake, Shelley, I said to myself. This is going to be an In-A-Gadda-Da-Vida, long day.

I called my boss, then my mom, and then friends seeking pity. The long ride turned into, "I am so alone in this journey of life...."

It was Friday and people weren't into this buzzkill stuff, so I quickly zoned in on the tunes and had that almost Harman

Kardon-like sound system turned up with the windows open and the breeze blowing through the flowing locks of my hair...oh, okay whatever, Hare Krishna scalp.

I thought this morning I would be writing about the fact that super cool guys always sit next to me on airplanes, and this trip was no exception. I thought it always happened because I am so sexy and cute but realized it's because I'm petite and am the perfect seat companion for any overweight, hunky or husky dude. Well, maybe it's partly because I'm cute...

Any hubris, I thought I would also write about texting pictures of random people in the airport to my friend and making up stories about them, like the man feeding his wife McDonald's to absolve his own guilt. Or maybe I was going to write about the hotel pillows smelling like dirty hair...nope.

I thought about stopping at the famous Wisconsin cheese shop for a photo-op, but I'm lactose intolerant. Hmmm, how about a photo-op in a hunting jacket from the truck shop, but was afraid I would want to buy one and, as far as I know, hunting jackets are not quite a business expense.

Any highway, I drove the shit out of that minivan for nine hours, told the pretend kids to "keep it down," sang my heart out along with Pearl Jam, Linkin Park and Led Zeppelin. I only stopped twice for gas and to pee. Lunch was peanuts, pork rinds and a diet Mountain Dew. I had this! I was singing, the colors were beautiful, I was the leader of the far left lane, and I was heading home.

I dropped off the minivan and with luggage in tow, met my friends, sang one karaoke song, went home and slept in my own bed.

Thanks to you I'm much obliged, such a pleasant stay...

CHAPTER 47

Miss Diagnosed

In honor of Mental Health Awareness Month. I am not mental health professional. This is simply my experience.

What is it this time? Maybe F41.1—Generalized anxiety disorder, or F43.23—Anxiety disorder and depressed mood, or perhaps F50.00 —Anorexia nervosa, unspecified, or F43.10— Post-traumatic stress disorder, unspecified.

Let's see, through the years, my various behavioral health insurance carriers received claims for 90791 Psychological diagnostic interview without medical services, and 90837 Individual Psychotherapy. In addition, a myriad of billing codes coinciding with residential treatment for disordered eating. Of course, all these ICD-10 Codes for Behavioral Health all begin with the letter F, as in:

- Fucked-up
- Failure

- Fix me
- Fragile
- Fractured
- Fragmented
- Father Issues
- Feed me

The list of antidepressants and antianxiety medications prescribed throughout the years jumbled together could make an amazing word search puzzle:

Prozacwellbutrintrazadoneeffexorlex
proluvoxpaxilzoloftviibryd

What word did you find first? The first word I see is "well," and this I wasn't, according to all of those F codes.

For most of my life, I've felt as if I were shattered pieces of broken glass held together by glue that never dried, a sort of Humpty Dumpty. I felt disintegrated, pieces of myself were constantly falling off. I sometimes picked up these broken pieces and attempted to restick them to the wet glue of me and watch them inevitably fall off again, leaving a trail of shards in brokenness. There was this mind and this body, and I could never see myself as the sum of all those parts, never mind anything to do with my perpetually emotionally stabbed and broken heart.

I existed through the lens of gray. If you bothered to ask me what I truly wanted for my life, after I yelled, "I wish I was dead," or "I want a lobotomy," or "*Nuuthiiiing*," I might be able to utter a tear-filled plea, "I just want a sense of peace."

Living inside this head was a torture of endless looping thoughts and self-hatred. Like many women, my suffering manifested itself through my relationship with my body that transcended self-hatred into self-destruction. There's no need to go into any more detail about what it was like. What I do want to offer is that there is hope.

No one ever told me I had a choice about the thoughts in my head. Instead, I was just a bunch of ICD-10 codes along with copays and prescriptions.

> I lived in desperation the
> next pill would cure me
> the next therapist would fix me,
> Jesus would save me,
> affirmations would transform me.

I didn't know the cure for my suffering wasn't out there. I didn't know that I wasn't broken. I didn't know that this one breath would save my life.

In retrospect, I don't believe there was ever any sort of chemical imbalance. From an early age, for many reasons, I developed a conditioned physiological response to react to every thought as if it was the truth without any sort of a pause button between the thought and the reaction. For me, each emotion engrossed me, encompassed me, became who I was at that given moment. I was racked with guilt, remorse, fear and regret. I numbed myself every way I could. I was suffering. I didn't know I wasn't stuck, and I didn't know I had a choice. I went for zero to crisis in seconds.

I grew out of many of the self-damaging behaviors but the emotional imbalance and ruminating thoughts only seemed to accelerate. More prescriptions, more therapy, more F codes...

The hope for me came a few years ago in the form of a mindfulness-based stress reduction program. Soon after, no more F codes, no more prescriptions. The potential benefits of mindfulness-based stress reduction, as tested in scientific studies, include pain relief, stress reduction, improved sleep, depression relapse prevention, and cognitive improvement.

I've deepened my mindfulness practice over the years and for me, because of this life-giving, transformative practice, my default state is now joy. I'm able to hold space for my emotions without becoming them. I'm able to observe my thoughts with curiosity and interest without reacting to them except on rare occasions. To this day, I often have disparaging thoughts about my body image yet I'm now able to practice self-compassion, accept myself with kindness, and let go even if I have to mindfully practice this throughout the day. I know that everything is impermanent. I can sense deep appreciation and love for myself and have an ever expanding heart of compassion for others. I know I am whole.

I've learned this one truth—pain is inevitable, suffering is optional.

Shattered shards, broken glass
Kicked in heart, fell on ass
Pieces of myself, I once knew
Corners broken, held by glue
Done dying,
The glue is drying
(2013)

Perhaps there is something I've shared here that you can relate to, or provides a spark of hope. If so, please reach out to me. I promise to have a call with you, to hold space for you, to be a resource for you.

May you be free from inner and outer harm.

May you sense your own wellspring of hope, healing and wholeness.

May you live with ease.

May you dwell in the awareness and truth of love.

I hesitated to publish this piece, as if showing up at an often stigmatized level of vulnerability will somehow diminish my value as a capable professional, however, my compassion for the suffering of others won out in an instant.

I'm committed to the continuous study and practice of mindfulness and have dedicated my career as a speaker and workshop facilitator extending an inclusive and accessible invitation to explore this transformative practice.

CHAPTER 48

Moving

I just counted. Holy U-Haul, I have moved eighteen times since 1991. Unbelievable.

I know it sounds like a lot but I have had more boyfriends, ran more marathons, had more hairdressers, hair colorists and nervous breakdowns but less deaths, less jobs, and less health concerns, so that's good right? I may be breaking even at men's boxer shorts acquired from ex-boyfriends, though.

Any homewrecker, the reason this came up in my weird mind is because I am embarking on my nineteenth move this Friday. I am moving to a different floor in my building with a balcony to make my petite apartment less dormesque. Do I think I will be there long term? No.

Do I foresee a move within the next year? You bet your bubble wrap, number twenty is right around the corner.

Maybe California? You can find me with love in my eyes and flowers in my hair.

Any packing tape, the good thing is I pretty much got rid of everything I owned a few years ago, so now I travel pretty light. The only things of value are my grandmother's armoire and an oriental rug that belonged to my mom. Other than that, thousands of dollars' worth of pantyhose and stockings. I seem to be incapable of getting rid of them. Can someone please do a hosiery intervention on me?

One of the most important keepsakes I have is a pink toy pony. His name is The Pony. He is a gender-confused plastic pony covered with pink felt. Someone I loved very much gave him to me. This someone called me before my forty-eighth birthday and said, "I have a surprise for you."

I said, "What is it? A Pony?"

He said "Yes, Shelley it's a pony."

Holy schoolgirl giggle, sure enough, at dinner in a very elegant restaurant, he presented me with a gift-wrapped box. When I opened it, there was The Pony!

Somehow, I quickly determined The Pony was really a he, and he came with decorations. I decorated him with my initials and the initials of the one I loved encircled by a heart.

I then took the marker and wrote on his butt, "No horse shit."

The Pony went to Florida, Asheville, Vegas, New York and many other places with us. He was the symbol of our love and our family. The Pony is now here with me in Chicago in a drawer. I see him once in a while and am flooded with emotions, some devastating, some wistful, and some beyond beautiful.

The other possession I have is Monk Monk, my forty-two-year-old sock monkey who is world famous for his duet with me, Linkin Park's "Burn it Down" on YouTube, as well as my black and white selfie.

Me, my rescue dog Potato, The Pony, and Monk Monk are my weird family. We are all here, and we are all safe. We are so well loved and blessed.

> It doesn't matter where you live
> because home isn't a place.
> Home is where you are.

Love,

Shelley

"In my Room"

↓ my fantasy bedroom

↓ Possibilty lives in my Bedroom where the Carpet matches the drapes

Dreamy Canopy Bed

Collage version of Monk Monk

Substitute for pee on the Carpet Yorkies

preferred Barbies over dolls with their major influence on my Self loathing

CHAPTER 49

My first marathon

Zing zap zing zap all night long. Like many, I tossed and turned. It was the night before my first marathon. It wasn't just the nerves about the race, I had recently begun bleaching my teeth for my upcoming wedding and those little bleach trays I wore at night could cut a bitch! I don't know if you have ever bleached your teeth but let me tell you, it can make you feel like little razor-sharp lightning bolts are going up and through the nerves of your teeth. Anybody cringing about now?

This was a huge day for me. I had quit smoking almost exactly one year before and now I was running my very first marathon. I knew this was going to be my goal when I decided to put down the cowboy killers.

My dad had been a marathoner and I thought it was so amazing. I also thought, as any daughter with daddy issues, this would be the thing that would make him proud of me and love me more! Holy hullabaloo! I was excited, terrified, anxious and exhausted all at the same time.

HOW (sob, hyperventilate), IS (gasping for breath) THIS, THIS, THIS (gasp) SUPPORT? Wendi Brown was on the other end of the phone trying to understand me as I gasped out the words while stammering, stuttering, sobbing, snorting and hyperventilating.

I had finished my first marathon, and it was an amazing experience. See how I made that description short? "Amazing experience," like it was a great meal. That's because I don't remember that much about the race but I do remember what happened after I finished.

After receiving my medal, I staggered to the tent assigned to my training group. My mom and dad were there waiting for me but this guy, who I will just call my fiancé, because he was, was nowhere to be found. After about thirty minutes, my happiness started to turn to little whimpers. Now this was 2001, and not everyone had a cellphone but eventually I did find someone who let me borrow theirs.

Ring ring. I was calling my house.

"Hello?" said the fiancé.

"Why aren't you here?" I asked in quiet disbelief

"I couldn't find the tent," he replied a little agitated.

"Well, did you ask somebody?" I retorted incredulous.

"Just come home." He hung up.

Holy hysteria. I went into total meltdown mode.

"Call off the wedding! Call off the wedding!"

My poor parents took me home as I inconsolably sobbed in the back seat. I asked my dad to stop at Starbucks on the way and get me a soy latte. Dad came back to the car, handed me the coffee. "Is it soy?" I asked.

That non-soy latte went airborne and splattered about a half a block down the street. The frustration of the situation coupled with my inability to be consoled was a bit much for poor Dad.

I got home, walked past my fiancé and straight to the tub. He walked in. "Congratulations," he said.

I didn't say a word. I struggled to get out of the tub, threw on some clothes and proceeded to limp away from home. I took myself to breakfast, sat alone with my victory medal around my neck and sobbed over my eggwhite omelet. I then staggered over to the park, sat on a bench and cried more.

My mom kept calling and I just keep saying, "Call off the wedding."

I called Wendi and some other friends. After about eight hours, I returned home.

It took a few days for me to embrace the victory, the wedding was beautiful and I went on to run many more races.

Please ask for directions. I love you.

CHAPTER 50

My mom is a B-A-D-A-S-S

Several years ago, my late father, my sister and I found ourselves sharing a hotel room in Baltimore. We didn't know that tiny little room would be our home for a month, nor did we know we would basically be living in Maryland, renting a condo for the next few months while my mother clung to life in a medically-induced coma. We didn't know that our daily trip to the ICU at Hopkins would become almost routine aside from the terrorizing infection that had the doctors perplexed and my mother's petite body fighting for life.

Every day we went to the ICU. Watching the monitors was liking watching a rollercoaster ride. Watching my mom swell with edema to the point where she was unrecognizable was nothing less than horrifying. Every night we would return to our little hotel room, my sister and I sharing one of the double beds, my dad in other until we got the condo.

I think we had been in that hotel room for about a month when my dad flew home to Chicago for twenty-four hours to take care of something urgent. I was running a fever and stayed back while my Aunt Sandy and my sister left for the hospital. They had literally just walked out of the hotel room when the phone rang. It was the doctor.

"You need to get here. We are losing her."

I don't remember if those were his exact words, but somehow I caught up with my sister and aunt.

The next thing I remember, I was instructed by a social worker to say goodbye to my mother. I remember it in great detail. About twenty years ago, it was one of the most gutwrenching, anguishing day of my life (my father passed several years later, hence the "one of the").

She didn't die.

It's not like one day she was just fine. It was a long, slow haul in every imaginable way, emotionally, physically, and mentally. My parents even traded homes with their friends (thank you, Marilyn Schanze) for a couple months, as they had a townhouse and their friends had a condo. After a couple months, my father would take my mom to the house to painstakingly practice climbing stairs. She literally couldn't even lift her hand at first, as her muscles were so atrophied.

One funny side note, after my mom was out of the coma, she had ICU psychosis. She thought there was a conspiracy to kidnap her from the hospital. She also thought I was married to Dan Rather (she was trying to control everything as usual— she knows damn well it was always Bill Kurtis for me).

Today my mother is alive and well, spirited, unsinkable, breast cancer survivor, ovarian cancer survivor, meningitis survivor and survivor of a crazy daughter.

Okay, my mom is a BADASS!!!

Thinking of all of you who have lost your mothers, thinking of you who wanted to be mothers and never had the opportunity, thinking of you who are mothers who have lost children, and thinking of those women who are battling major illnesses and thinking of their families. My prayers are with you all.

Happy Mother's Day to my mom and to all of you BAD-ASS mommas out there, including those whose children are the four-legged kind.

" Coffee is my favorite food "

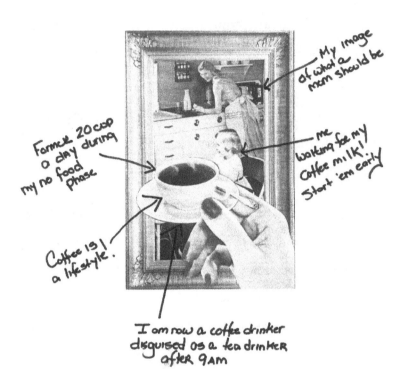

My image of what a mom should be

me waiting for my coffee milk! Start 'em early

Former 20 cup a day during my no food phase

Coffee is a lifestyle!

I am now a coffee drinker disguised as a tea drinker after 9 AM

CHAPTER 51

Naked & afraid

I was told what to bring but had no idea what it was going to be like. I didn't even Google it because somehow I wanted to keep the experience pure. Then, about three hours later, I stood there naked and afraid.

They were many. They were naked. They were unafraid, women and children, all naked. It was strange to see so many naked people of all shapes and sizes without a hint of self-consciousness.

I could feel their stares, like daggers piercing the heart of my back tattoo while I tried to cover my nakedness with a towel about the size of a napkin.

He told me we were going to a spa, to bring my clothes, and to make sure to bring socks because the sauna floors are very hot. I packed my backpack with my clothes and some makeup, and of course the requisite socks.

He picked me up, I got into the car, and we drove towards O'Hare. We exited off the Kennedy after passing the iconic Superdawg on Milwaukee Ave and the bowling alley where I had recently bowled with the guy who stole Christmas (see Weird Girl archives) until we reached a strip mall. Then I saw it. The outside was as big as a six-theatre cinema. The big red letters spelling out KING SPA. I wasn't sure what I was in for, but knew I would be writing about it.

We entered the building where two women stood behind a desk. We checked in and were given bracelets with a number and a key. A nice Korean woman was kind enough to escort me to the women's locker room.

I was told to take off my shoes. She asked me, "Is that your husband?"

I replied, "No."

She said "Who is he to you?"

I said, "A friend."

I wasn't sure if that was a cultural question or if she was just curious.

We entered the large locker room where I was given a pair of pink shorts and matching top. I passed by a few women sitting on the left, each wearing some huge brown tent looking things. I headed toward my assigned locker. He had told me they would give me a cute little pink outfit to wear. He left out the GINORMOUS part.

The women then asked me, "Do you have underwear?"

I replied "No."

She said "Sanitation not so good."

I'm thinking, great. Total cooties in the ginormous pink shorts.

I took a quick pitstop to the restroom where I was able to read on the back of the stall door about how I could steam my vagina with a sitz bath. There was even a photo of a smiling woman in the same brown tent-looking thing with just her head sticking out of the tent while her vag was being steamed. I read about how this Korean treatment is used for reducing stress, fighting infections, helping with fertility and hemorrhoids, providing relief from menstrual cramps and backache, and minimizing cysts.

I met him in the unisex room. He was in shorts and a top just like mine except his was gray. The unisex room featured about a hundred huge pink chairs, checkers game stations, and a café. There were a bunch of doors to different rooms, the Gold Room, Amethyst Room, Fire Room, and more.

We started out in one of the rooms, a 140-degree sauna. I loved it. It was really relaxing. You pick up a normal size towel, enter the room, lay it on the mat and there are wood things for your feet and head to rest on. We stayed there for a bit, took a break and went to the Gold Room, a cooler sauna at 120 degrees, with a gold-leaf pyramid sealing. Some young Korean guys were sitting on mats texting and a woman was reading a Korean newspaper.

They all left after a bit and an American woman entered. After she asked us to be quiet, we left the Gold Room and went on to the Fire Room. The Fire Room was HELL, it was so hot you could cook a meal in there. I covered my face with my T-shirt and ran out within minutes. Good thing the Ice Room was next door.

We walked around and he informed me that this place is open twenty-four-hours, that those who drink come here to detox, and that illicit sexual acts have reportedly taken place in some of those spa rooms.

We ended up in the Oxygen Room where a sign told us to refrain from any type of public displays of affection. I said that this would be the perfect refuge during the wintertime and can only describe it as an Asian foot massage store met Las Vegas and took steroids.

We decided it was time to finish up our time at King Spa. We agreed to meet in twenty minutes after using the pools in our respective locker rooms. I especially was looking forward to the cold plunge.

I walked back into the locker room and that's when it happened.

I asked for a towel and was given one the size of a napkin. Everyone was walking around naked except for the women getting their vaginas steamed. I was trying to be comfortable, yet don't particularly feel comfortable walking naked around a bunch of people. I don't mind that they are naked, I mind that I am naked, even though in my younger years I went through a brief phase of thinking being a stripper could be a very profitable venture.

Any just me, I used my napkin-towel to try to cover up which was completely ridiculous, and headed toward the cold pool where I was promptly joined by three naked little girls.

I decided I had enough of being naked and went back into the main locker room where I got yelled at because I had accidently put my flip-flops on after stripping down. I don't know, maybe to look taller naked?

Any hoo ha, I would go back in a tattooed heartbeat naked and unafraid, packing a towel along with me.

"Neither Elizabeth nor her pug are Vegan"

CHAPTER 52

Namaleaving

Woman walking down the street with a yoga mat protruding from large purse-thing as if shouting to the world, "Look at me, I just worked out."

Me, shouting to the world but really in my head, "And now you are drinking a Frappuccino?"

I have been getting messages seemingly from everywhere including outerspace to do yoga, not because I need more inner peace but because my body is typically in discomfort and my range of motion bending forward extends to my ability to barely reach the middle of my thighs.

Any high calorie after yoga beverage, I have yoga issues. My problem with yoga is not just the fact that after years of running and back surgery I am stiff as a tongue depressor, I simply have a disdain for other people's feet and yoga pants.

Holy camel digit! Couldn't do it. Those two combined just creep me the fuck out and I go CRAY.

You, millions of men who have dated me, and those of you who were fortunate enough to be bedded down by me, are well aware that if one touches me with their feet, I go insane and scream as if stabbed in the eye with a Bic pen. Do people really use Bic pens anymore? Does anyone use a ballpoint pen except for the free branded pens in hotels and nail salons?

I have size eight foot and frankly, at five-foot-one, that makes me a hobbit. Okay, hobbit minus the hair covering both my toes and feet.

Any Helm's Deep, if I do yoga, will I start meditating with Oprah and Deepak? Will I stop believing in God and worship a mass-produced porcelain figure? Will I mistake that zit on my forehead for a third eye? Will having my ass up in the air no longer be a sacred private matter?

I put on my pseudo-yoga pants, an old pair of running leggings with a nice gaping hole in the stitching near my outer thigh, and hurried to a place called Yoga Now with a sense of urgency because the name itself made me a little anxious.

The young woman at the front desk introduced me to the yoga instructor.

Yogi, "How are you feeling?"

Me, "Afraid."

Yogi, "Cool."

Me, "My lumbar spine is fused."

Yogi, "Cool. Where?"

Me, "L5/S1."

Yogi, "Cool."

The room has a distinct odor of, ah, yes, feet. Yogi kept talking, and talking, and talking. The entire practice was painful. Yogi tried to help modify every position for me. It was anything but cool. Yoga Now is icky, full of feet, I hurt and my back feels like it's on fire.

> Yoga,
> it causes great suffering.

Yogi, after class, "I think you should probably take private lessons, as we have to modify everything for you."

Me, "Cool." As if I can actually afford this painful torture in private.

Yoga Now will now be referred to as Yoga Not Now, Yoga Never, or Yoga Later.

In the words of a not so famous non-yogi weird girl who enjoys making up pretend yoga words: Sha Na Nee Na Na– Peace Be With You or Alyshenoo. May the wind be at your back.

Cool.

Namaleaving.

CHAPTER 53

No panties, no massage

I keep getting emails to meditate with Oprah and Deepak Chopra. When I see the email's subject line in my inbox, I try to quickly delete but it's too late. All I can hear is Oprah's booming voice belting out, "Now it's time to meditate everybody! Look under your seats. Everyone gets their very own Deepak!"

Frankly, I get a little stressed. Meditation over...

Jan Brown, "Do you take your underwear off when you get a massage?"

Me, "You do realize that you keep fueling my writing, don't you?"

Jan Brown, "Seriously, do you take your underwear off when you get a massage?"

Me, "Yes, of course. I want them to get my ass really good, Mom. Why are you asking?"

Besides being a strange question, I was so excited to have this conversation happen for realz. Not quite as good as the woman whose boyfriend grew up in the circus, *butt* . . . (tee hee). Apparently my weird mom's weird boyfriend thinks this is very wrong.

Any Hane's, my weird mom has a massage therapist in San Diego. She told me he is really good and used to work for the Padres. I don't know if my mom's criteria for choosing a masseuse had to do with the major leagues or not.

Any Hall of Famer, one day my mom's eighty-four year-old boyfriend was waiting for her after the massage and when they came out of the room, the massage therapist hugged and kissed my mom on the lips.

Are you picturing this? My mom's eighty-four-year-old boyfriend goes ballistic on the forty-three-year-old massage therapist, and they almost get in a fistfight. My mom just walks away and goes in the shower.

My mom now has a female massage therapist and I really don't know if she keeps her panties on or not. My mom's boyfriend is still upset...to be continued.

CHAPTER 54

Nun

So I have writer's block and it's giving me a headache. I walked around at lunch looking for inspiration and saw a nun.

Nuns always evoke totally weird thoughts in my mind. Like, I don't understand why they can't update the nun outfit and habit. I think the habit is only the head thingy. Is it a habit because they have to wear it habitually? I'm not saying they should make it sexy or anything, but if Joseph wore a coat of many colors, I would think Jesus might like his brides in some fuchsia or teal. I get they are supposed to look plain and chaste, but there's no harm in color. Didn't God create the rainbow? Now the nuns just look like fifty shades of grey.

I also wonder if the clergy has some type of supply chain management where they get the ugly black shoes and nude pantyhose in bulk? Are the nuns wearing pantyhose or do they wear knee-highs? Do they all have to wear the same panties? I know they don't go to Victoria's Secret. Do they get an allowance? Can they spend it on whatever they want? Do they have a curfew?

Any undergarment, I always smile at nuns and for some reason feel like if I smile at them, they'll think I'm a good girl and didn't do all those naughty things I did in the past. Since they are closer to God, do they know the truth?

I don't say, "Hello, Sister." I usually just quietly say, "Hi," like I'm demure. After all the stories I've heard about mean nuns in Catholic schools, I feel like I have to smile or else.

Any promiscuous early adulthood, I recently took a picture of some nuns. One of them knew I was up to no good and the other gladly posed. I was so close to asking if we could all take a holy selfie but then thought WWJD. I think Jesus would have taken selfies. Think about it. Jesus would have had a selfie of the last supper on his Facebook page forever.

Holy fantastic monastic! I would love some type of communal living environment right about now. No, not like on a tour bus where you have to share a tiny smelly bathroom. Speaking of which, did you ever want to make a disclaimer after leaving a bathroom when someone else is waiting to use it, and you don't want them to think *that* was you? I know the answer and it's not nun of you!

I want to live in a community with all my closest friends, the ones who are near and those who have moved away, some ex-boyfriends, and the ones I haven't seen in years. It would be like Facebook in real life. We would have a rotating schedule of who can choose the music for that night, and we would all sing the songs that span our lifetime. Imagine a world where we don't catch up online...oops, waxing nostalgic.

Speaking of waxing, how many nuns get waxed? I bet nun!

I know I could find out everything I want to know about nuns if I were to look online. For instance, is it necessary to use a capitol "N" in the writing of this Weird Girl? I could find out but I took a vow not too...ever...swear to God...

Okay, this story had become a cloister fuck!!! I am going to go find a ruler...

I love you. Be good or else!

"Doris wonders who wouldn't wish for a big a Wiener?"

Who?

BigWiener: my dad used to go to the Vienna outlet & get the deformed rejects :(You should have seen them!

Doris must not be having much luck on Tinder

CHAPTER 55

Obsessions of the weird kind

I have a thing with coffee. It may be one of my favorite things in life bordering on obsession. I can't drink as much as I want anymore, yet I love everything about it.

My weird mom started me young on *coffee milk*, milk with sugar and maybe a tablespoon of coffee. I'm sure that was a fantastic idea. Maybe she thought I needed more energy? Well that's when it started.

My weird dad was obsessed with rye bread and Nathan's hotdogs, and would bring them back in his suitcase from New York when he visited family in New Jersey. He must've washed his clothes from the suitcase. I would hate to think of my weird dad, a veterinarian, smelling like hot dogs.

Any hotdog, back to the point. Well, maybe not. I went through a time when I was obsessed with Hot Tamales, the red cinnamon chewy candy likely to take out a filling. I used to hoard boxes of Hot Tamales as if they were going to be discontinued, or I might suddenly develop agoraphobia and wouldn't be able to leave the house to get my fix.

I then went through a phase when I was obsessed with flavored Tootsie Rolls, the vanilla ones in particular. After my former mother-in-law bought me a five-pound tub, five pieces a night turned into a gutful of globby gloop until I finally OD'd on them. I gave up candy for good after that.

Any Hot Tamale, before Starbucks, Peet's and Carribou, coffee was served in a regular cup and saucer and came in only one flavor—coffee. I liked it so much I got a tattoo of it, which is now covered up.

Do you remember Sanka, the dehydrated decaffeinated coffee that came in an orange bag? At restaurants, they gave you a metal decanter of hot water to add to the crystals, and violà. Instant coffee that tasted like crap.

Speaking of tasting like crap, when I was a little girl, my weird mom used to chew Carefree sugarless gum. It came in Bottom of a Purse flavor, or maybe that's just what I thought because she never chewed a whole stick. When I saw her chewing gum and would ask for some, she would dig through the bottom of her purse and give me some random torn piece of Carefree gum with purse lint attached. The end.

CHAPTER 56

Onethingwrong

Written before we knew Bill Cosby became that kind of Bill Cosby.

By Sunday I felt like I had finally done it. I had finally had the nervous breakdown to end all nervous breakdowns. This was it. I was going to combust into a million little pieces.

Well, that didn't happen. I just simply fell apart.

Everything was wrong, and the big kick in the ass was my wireless connection got screwed up. By the end of the day, I was trying to have the patience to understand this woman with a very heavy Asian dialect walk me through reconfigureing my TP-link WR741ND.

I tried to fix the issue myself for hours as my rescue dog Potato sat there and barked at me and then just decided to start biting me.

I guess because it was Labor Day, I couldn't get through to customer service until late last night and after the call with the cable provider.

I have an illness, Onethingiswrongsoeverythingiswrong Syndrome. It doesn't flair up that often, but once in a while it does and I've come down with it a couple times recently. It's totally icky. I went on a road trip with this syndrome all over ShelleyLand this weekend.

Sometimes when life gets crazy and I am under stress, I fail to see the obvious and make it about *everything*! The fact is that I have a rescue dog who has taken over my life. It's really stressful and he desperately needs training. I know he had good owners before me but they did not have a lot of time for him, which is why they gave him up.

PotatoLand must be a crazy place too. Maybe Potato has the Whoisthispersonwhodoesntknowwhatineed Syndrome. I know he's super cute, and I know we will be good for each other and it will take time. I also know I have no idea what I'm doing and he knows it, too.

So instead of it being about the obvious, it became *everything*. I am a horrible person, I am old, why did I move back to Chicago, why didn't I have children, why are there still mean girls in adulthood, why does calling the cable company make me want to slit my throat, I did something bad and that's why my internet isn't working...

Do you ever get like this? I hope I am not the only one who loses perspective.

I was beating the crap out of myself and feeling very childish when I said to myself, "You want to see people with problems? I'll show you people with problems," as if I had come from a made-for-TV movie with scripted lines from my actor parents. All of the sudden, Bill Cosby was going to show up on set as my crazy uncle and say something like, "When I was your age, we only had Jell-O pudding, and you think you have problems . . . ?"

If I were a TV show, who would I want my parents to be? Hmm, just trying to be age appropriate here...Judi Dench and Christopher Walkin? Jane Fonda and Jack Nicholson? Wait! Maybe Julie Andrews because she would be nurturing and could sing to me, and Dustin Hoffman because he seems to have the perfect combination of neurotic-laid back type of thing my real father had, although my dad was little bit more like Woody Allen accept for the...well, you know...

My dad had a strange saying that never failed to puzzle me yet provided humor and caused me to giggle. He would say, "Things just haven't been the same since the twins died."

I've got it! I think my dad should be played by the Most Interesting Man in the World, who actually is a Jewish American actor. After all, he can speak Russian…in French!

So after physically and emotionally feeling like I fell in a gutter full of glass shards, I went to bed and told Potato it was going to be alright. He agreed, and we went to sleep.

We are now registered for classes. Thank the good God! I am committed to falling in love with my dog and to learning how to make this relationship work.

Now there are still mean girls, but it's not personal. I don't think I am a horrible person, I'm glad I moved back to Chicago, my dog is really cute, I don't think I will ever enjoy calling the cable company. My parents were my parents, and Bill Cosby is not my uncle.

My dog and I need help but *everything* isn't wrong. The treatment for my syndrome is a healthy dose of perspective, a little bit of sleep, and the love I get from you.

Love,

Shelley

CHAPTER 57

On the edge of softness

I couldn't stop running my tongue over it. Back and forth again and again, my tongue explored the sharpness. There was something so compelling about the sensation. Why is that?

Oh, yeah, it's the edge. The rough, serrated, sharp edge.

This was just my tooth whose decades-old filling lost the battle to a frozen gluten-free, dairy-free, non-GMO, grass-fed whey protein chocolate protein bar packed with omega-3 that tasted like heaven to this nondairy, no sugar, gets hungover before finishing a half a drink, celiac, minimal cruciferous vegetable-consuming, bloated belly, 9 p.m. bedtiming, the age of the most iconic Chevy me.

Oh, and I can only have half the protein bar according to my nutritionist who is helping me mitigate all my non-ing and now, *now*, I can't eat the half bar from the freezer anymore, in case something even more egregious occur such as the dislodging of an old crown or, in my case, a crown not quite as old as an iconic Chevy and not quite as young as non-GMO. I have resigned myself to eating my half in its non-frozen form, which is—soft.

Soft. The mere thought of the word itself seems to ask for an apology, "I'm sorry. I'm just soft."

Soft brings images of toilet paper, babies bottoms, flaccid penises, and medical conditions described by using the highly underutilized word "stool."

Soft are body parts with undefined muscle tone, the fluffy grandma in a schmata, the rice pudding we eat when our wisdom teeth get pulled, and the I-was-once-a-vibrant-yellow-until-you-peeled-and-mashed-me banana.

I can handle soft in art, such as whimsy, yet I find aversion to sentiment unless it's joy, because joy has the energy to slap sap in the face!

The ever expanding circle of Kumbaya...sentiment...self-care, self-love, kindness, compassion, like being stuck in an elevator with Muzak and somehow the Muzak track gets stuck on a Michael Bublé song causing me the desire to throw myself head first into the gnarly angst of a disturbed refrain, "Down with the sickness."

Soft serve, soft porn, soft rock…

Edges aren't soft, and I knew from a young age that hard happens, like Ken coming home to Barbie from Nam minus a leg. Nowadays it's when I look in the mirror thinking, "Man, I look kind of sexy," followed by the game-over sneeze in my light-colored Lululemon's right before spin class.

What's so wrong with soft?

There are some good soft things like sheets, my favorite green dress circa 2007 laundered five million times, and my dog's fur.

I have this craving to be some ballbuster chick who, when you look at her, think, "She likes her rock hard, her cock hard, and her liquor harder," yet I know that this striving has everything to do with the what's lurking behind my softer feminine side.

Hard and edgy. I know them well. I sought them out, tried them on and wore them in the many forms so many of us do, from fuck me to fuck you, and everything in between.

"Are you softening?" asked a friend recently.

My reaction, "Oh shit! Got to shatter this hair like I fucked all night, rolled out of a gutter full of glass, and dyed it platinum. Where's my *edge*? Where's my hard?!"

I lay in bed, feel and tense my ass to assess if there's still some throw-me-against-the-wall, I-want-to-fuck-you-so-bad there. I get up, look in the mirror, pull at the top of my breasts, lift them up a couple inches higher to their allegedly former position, followed by the de rigueur pulling up the skin on my neck while pulling back my jawline for my coveting a lower face lift.

Walk away, laughing at myself saying, "Fuck it!" with a mischievous twinkle in my eye, some sort of digestive upset, boobs lifted in too tight of a sports bra.

Time to go get the filling replaced with something *harder*.

Living on the edge...

of softness...

CHAPTER 58

Ooops, there goes my vagina

Aging. How weird. If I could just look at it without judgment, it would be kind of funny, you know like practicing mindfulness, letting thoughts just float and pass like little butterflies, floating, floating, in the air across my mind. So how do I practice mindfulness around the thoughts about my aging vagina?

I'm here to tell you what the selfish women who have gone before us neglected to share. You may think that your highly coveted pussy is going to remain plump, pink forever, a peachy desirable treasure that men covet and wish to dive into. One word: Nope.

I knew I would need a lot of upkeep when it came to wrinkle prevention and, yes, I am a big fan of fillers and Botox. In fact, I would chest-bump for it in public with other willing women. However, I had no idea about the aging issues I would face with my lady parts.

After my total hysterectomy, I was concerned that my boyfriend could feel the vortex that recently contained my womb, as if his dick had an eye that could see this cavernous space and ask, "Where did it all go?"

I was concerned about gaining weight and getting the spare tire around my middle. Fortunately through the miracle of hormone replacement and dedication to fitness, those fears have been kept at bay. Nothing, however, has shaken my foundation quite like the physical and emotional pain of what has happened *down there*. Pubic hair used to be a chastity belt, and now it's a curtain trying to hide what's lurking behind it.

I have decided to use my voice to tell you stuff that you may not otherwise know. Not to scare you or make you feel bad, but to inform you so you're not totally taken by surprise as I have been. Maybe it's my own ignorance. Maybe it's lack of cable. After all, don't they talk about this shit on Dr. Oz? By the way, how many of us can relate to a person who would be an audience member of daytime talk show?

Any Oprah, she didn't even talk about this. By no means am I a professional, nor do I have the slightest bit of medical training. I'm just speaking from my own experience of looking down there and not knowing if what was happening to me was normal.

Fortunately, we live in an age where information is readily available to us, yet the information that's out there doesn't feel personal. In fact, it feels quite the opposite. I found myself asking my mother, "Why didn't you tell me my vagina would shrivel up and fall off?"

"I have cramps. I'm getting my period."

This was a friend's reply to my question when I asked her, "How are you today?"

Okay, want to hear something you may have thought but never wanted to utter out loud? I miss the smell of being a menstruating woman, the good smells, the icky smells, the pungent smells, the smell of myself at the gym that lingers for a moment after getting up from a bench, the unspoken sisterhood of asking a complete stranger, "Hey, do you have a tampon I can borrow?" As though you were going to return it. "Oh hey, here's your tampon back."

I'll even go so far as to tell you that I miss tasting my sexuality on a lover's face after...

There is no husband reassuring me that it's just not that important, and it doesn't help that I am barren with no children with which to measure time.

Perhaps the only solution is
mindfulness and acceptance.

Instead of butterflies floating through my mind, I can notice little aging vaginas floating past me and simply notice them with kindness and gentleness, without judgment.

CHAPTER 59

Pantyhose

At least a thousand dollars . . . I must have at least a thousand dollars' worth of pantyhose in my closet. I am by no means a hoarder. I just have a hard time throwing out anything that's in perfect condition and costs upwards of fifteen dollars.

Pantyhose back in the day were a rite of passage. I, for one, couldn't wait to wear pantyhose. I saw my mom take hers out of those plastic eggs and I was mesmerized.

I was allowed to wear only tights until about age twelve or thirteen. I don't remember the exact day, but do remember when my mom handed me my own egg ready to hatch into a grown-up pair of nude color pantyhose.

As the years went on, my little hatched pantyhoselings were no longer good enough for me. I started craving better pantyhose, like DKNY, Calvin Klein, etc.

Like many of you, the anticipation and excitement of putting on the twenty-dollar DKNYs with a new dress would be short-lived thanks to a snagged fingernail. Into the garbage, you stupid crappy twenty-dollar piece of shit! That's why I had to buy two or three at a time. Sixty dollars' worth of pantyhose sometimes for just one night. My coming of age and opening of eggs soon turned pain into a very unpleasant, costly bane of my existence.

Any hose, I have at least a thousand dollars' worth of pantyhose in a plastic container prison in my closet, and they can't get out. They really aren't the kind of thing to donate. Am I right? That would be like donating underwear. I think I should throw them out. Will somebody help me through this? I need help and, no, I am not a hoarder and, yes, I would make a frickin' cool art piece if I had those darn plastic eggs.

If you have to wear pantyhose today, I am sorry.

Love,

Shelley

CHAPTER 60

Paper towelism

It always comes down to one thing, doesn't it? Something happened when you were young that shaped who you are.

Maybe an important someone said something that stuck in your mind and now defines the way you feel about yourself and your self-worth. Something like your father didn't show affection, your sister was your mother's favorite, and so on. Even though you don't consciously think about it, that one thing affects the daily choices you make.

For some people, that indelible thing or situation caused them to use alcohol, drugs, sex, food, or worse, videogames. You may never ultimately get to the root of why, but awareness and accountability are the first step.

For me, all roads lead to Paper Towelism and let me tell you, this is a literal and figurative syndrome. You may even know someone who is afflicted by it. In fact, the significance of Paper Towelism in my life is evidenced by the fact that I have written about this in the past.

"Hi, my name is Shelley, and I am addicted to paper towels."

There, I've now said it publicly and really hope my story will help someone else.

I've spoken of my love for paper towels in the past as if nonchalantly talking about cookies or a Gin Ricky. I've been very casual about expressing this love, however, have come to realize it's not really love, it's an addiction.

Just as the alcoholic can't have just one drink, I can't have just three rolls.

I want to be very candid here, because this addiction has affected other areas of my life and certainly other people in my life who continue to support and enable my addiction by driving me places like Target, physically carrying and even paying for my addiction. I make up excuses at checkout lines like, "Can you imagine what it's like living with five little ones in a studio apartment?"

I have openly and publicly toted large, cumbersome six-packs on buses, trains, and taxis.

This problem has now transcended to Larrabars, toilet paper, and apples, as well as to two other strange but definitely related manifestations: vacuum lines and garbage.

I learned that most people throw garbage in the garbage can, however, when I put a new bag in the garbage can, I don't want to get the new bag dirty by throwing in refuse such as food items left on a dinnerplate. Typically, if the garbage bag is relatively new and we've finished dinner, I take out a grocery bag and put the food scraps in it to avoid putting them in the new, clean garbage bag.

After doing *the work*, as in years of therapy and other types of help, unlike others, I have been able to get to the *why*.

I have Paper Towelism because my father didn't love me enough and left when I was really young, my mom was never there for me because she had to work the third shift; my sister was messy and sneezed on my carpet; my first-grade teacher said something so mean that I can't bring it to immediate recall; I was bullied as a child; I came from a chaotic home; I experienced lots of neglect and abuse; drugs were rampant; my grandfather was gay but not allowed to be out at that time.

I shoved all this down with sheet after sheet, sometimes after a half-sheet. So, it totally makes sense that this would happen, right?

I now know I'm responsible for my own behavior and for keeping my side of the street clean (metaphorically).

I know I have to be able to walk into Target and leave without a twelve-pack. I need to look at three rolls not as half empty but as half full. I need to count my blessings because many people around the world and even in this country are forced to buy generic, or maybe never have the opportunity to have one roll at all.

I am growing and learning and accepting the fact that although that stuff happened to me, or for me, as I have come to understand, and even though I didn't receive my first hug until I was sixteen from *that* man, and I never really experienced love until later in life, three rolls of paper towels in a six-pack is not half empty, it's Bounty-full.

CHAPTER 61

Play guitar

My first summer camp experience, however traumatic, was slightly better than the latter years when I won the Crying Towel. You guessed it, the award for the camper who cried the most.

I was nine years-old, all long-haired, freckly faced innocence when I first went to camp. It was my first experience in a log cabin where young upper-middle-class mostly Jewish girls were taught foreign things like sharing. We were also taught how to sweep, which many of us would never do again for years to come, if ever. We had a bucket of red chunky things that looked like chopped pencil erasers we scattered on the floor, and they would aid in grabbing strands of hair, bugs, and miscellany. I don't remember how seven or eight of us were able to share one bathroom without barfing. At least it was indoors.

Besides my Precious Moments stationary (the odd kinda doll, kinda angel, kinda fucked-up looking figurine with the giant head and one strand of gentile blonde hair and teardrop-shaped eyes), my fondest memories were when I'd become so homesick and cry so inconsolably that this one counselor, a chubby, ponytailed, acne-faced teenager, would take me to the mess hall in the middle of the night to give me milk and cookies to shut me the fuck up. Well, it worked. I still don't know which one of us wanted the cookies more.

The other memory is when a beautiful older girl named Andy, a gorgeous teenager who already had breasts, brought her six-string nylon guitar to our cabin.

Andy. God, how I wished I could be Andy.

With her dark hair, dark skin, and dark eyes, when she started strumming her guitar, magic happened. Her pretty voice and her strumming of 57th Bridge Street song by Simon and Garfunkel changed my life forever. I was feeling groovy and was on a quest to be groovy.

Along came Mr. Norrel, Andy's guitar teacher. Far out! Just the thought of this memory makes me feel groovy! He smelled like unwashed hair and whatever breakfast foods were left in his dark scraggly beard. The entire block of kids would stop in their tracks for a moment, as if frozen in time, when

"Shelley, it's time for your guitar lesson," came blaring out of nowhere. Was it God? Was it Checkpoint Charlie? No, it was Mr. Norrel turning the corner in his broken-down banana yellow Pacer.

"Breaker one-nine!" The speaker connected to his CB radio was used to announce to the entire neighborhood it was time to for me to get my ten-year-old groovy on.

Mr. Norrel and I would enter Eva's room. Eva was our Alice of the Brady Bunch uniform-wearing live-in maid. She corrected me from calling her negro and said, "I am Black." She really did wear the same exact powder-blue uniform as Alice did on TV, complete with nude stockings and white shoes.

Eva was usually pissed and exclaimed "Sheet!" often, but I was her favorite and she gave me the coveted Oscar Meyer Weiner whistle because she liked me better than my snarky sister. I wonder if it was because I sang to her and told her I wrote the song "Puppy Love," or maybe it was just by default because I was my parents' favorite too, even if I was a faux lyricist.

Well, my first song was not groovy at all, but I sang it loud and proud. It was later when I realized these two idiots, Frankie and Johnny, were apparently lovers who promised to be true to each other but scumbag Johnny somehow ended up hooking up with Nelly Bly at some bar and doing Frankie wrong, so Frankie shoots asshole-cheater Johnny dead.

Where was my, "Slow down, you move too fast, you gotta make the mornin' laaa-ast?"

Mr. Norrell was feeding my mind with immoral songs about revenge and there ain't no good men.

Really? Really, Mr. Norrel?

Soon after mastering this nightmare of a song, the big day came. It was really happening! I was going to be like Andy, grow breasts, be beautiful and maybe someday visit a younger girl's camp cabin to have her worship me in all of my puberty enhanced splendor. It's time to *feel groovy*!

CHAPTER 62

Sequins

I am not proud of it, but figure the statute of limitations based how many years ago it was kind of erases the fact that it actually occurred.

Once upon a time before my moral compass pointed in the right direction, I had a sugar daddy. I was a kept woman.

A *kept* woman is one who is maintained in a comfortable or even lavish lifestyle by a wealthy man so she'll be available for his sexual pleasure. Such a woman could move between the roles of a mistress and a courtesan, depending on her situation and environment.

Okay, so he wasn't exactly a big Costco-size Sugar Daddy, more like a couple of packets in a bowl at your local diner sugar daddy. My surroundings were not exactly lavish, however I moved from my parent's Gold Coast townhouse up the street three blocks to a furnished apartment. I know you are thinking "Wow, knowing Shelley, it was probably real fancy!"

No, not quite.

I had no idea how to have my own bank account or even how to pay rent, but this man who kept me for his sexual pleasure basically took care of it all, paid my rent, and gave me an allowance. Far from extravagant, the apartment had brown furniture, mustard-yellow kitchen appliances, and a Murphy bed stained with pee. How's that for kept?

Any roach motel, I had to keep the lights on in the kitchen to keep those disgusting bugs in their hiding place.

I really loved this man. Any daddy issues, he was much older than me, about fifteen years. He had a cool 1961 Cadillac Fleetwood with aqua-blue leather interior and matching aqua-blue exterior. He would drive me to places mysterious and foreign, like the suburbs, while listening to Lou Rawles.

This man was the first person I ever met with a cellphone, which was pretty much the size of box of a Kleenex cut in half lengthwise. He liked to buy me clothes and often wanted me to dress more mature. It was the eighties, and I guess my neon-green fingerless gloves and off-the-shoulder sweatshirts were not very ladylike.

For my birthday, he bought me a fire engine-red backless sequin dress with huge shoulder pads that I proudly wore with my new black patent stilettos, and of course really expensive pantyhose. It was like my Bob Mackie dreams had come true!

We had a very romantic dinner during my special weekend, which we spent at the Pfister Hotel in Milwaukee. On the way home, he surprised me by pulling into a strip mall where he had picked out a short fox fur coat. Sure wish I had that to wear with the red sequined dress.

After a couple years, I decided it was time to be unkept (as opposed to *unkempt*). It was a hard breakup. My dad came over and commiserated. We sat on the brown carpet drinking scotch I had been given by a master blender wearing a kilt who probably would have *kept* me differently. Years later, I gave the dress to a crossdresser whom I am certain looked equally stunning, and I accidently set the fur coat on fire when I threw it over a chair one day and apparently over the floor lamp as well, which ultimately caused the demise of the fox that was already dead in the first place.

I thought about this yesterday as I sat there swiping left while living in the world of Nope. My birthday is next Tuesday. No sequins, no sugar daddy, no fox fur, and no more swiping left. I deleted the app. Just happy to be.

"Edna Can't decide"

CHAPTER 63

She's arrived

It looked like Keith Moon had stayed in that room minus the empty whiskey bottles, smashed TV, and fag butts. She had been in that room for less than twenty-four hours. How did she do it?

Weirdapedia for my young readers:

Keith Moon—Self-destructive crazy over the top English rock drummer for the band The Who. Died of a drug overdose.

Fag butt—Snubbed out end of a previously smoked fag.

Fag—British term for a cigarette.

The Who—One of the all-time greatest rock bands that I hope to never hear in a remix.

The black Cadillac Escalade pulled up to the front of my building. Clad in her ever-present latex gloves and large sunglasses, we greeted as the driver struggled to unload her four giant suitcases. Not surprising for her, or for someone traveling abroad for two weeks. She saw me looking at it and exclaimed, "Don't you fucking write about this!"

I couldn't take my eyes off it. It was the size of a king-size pillow. I just stared awestruck and transfixed. Holy handbag! My tiny weird mom had this black leather thing hanging off her shoulder, and it wasn't another piece of luggage. It was her purse. I could use it for a weekend trip and easily name five male friends who could use it for a week-long trip to Europe. I finally stopped staring and we headed up to the guest suite.

"Mom, let me set your expectations about the guest suite," I said on the phone several weeks before. "It's not glamorous by any means." I was talking about the guest suite we rented for her in my building.

"It will be fine, Shelley," she said.

Before her arrival, I purchased 7th Generation cleaner, paper towels, bottles of water and placed the items along with extra blankets in the suite. My guess was one night in this unit with its rented furniture, unidentifiable odor and whatever germs she could find with her travel-size blue light.

I spent the next morning looking for hotels. We packed her four giant suitcases and her mutant purse and headed for a hotel...

Actually, before we headed for the hotel, I headed to Willow Creek. Any Holy Spirit, I couldn't get there fast enough. I sat down and was so happy to be there because I always feel better and more peaceful after I get fed some spiritual food.

Not so fast.

Right in front of me was a young man with some sort of disorder that caused him to obsessively pick at his face and then look at the pickage. At first, I thought he was crying but no, he kept picking and looking, picking and looking. I was trying to figure out how to cover my right eye so I didn't have to see him pick and look.

Somehow I managed to cover my right eye but then on the far side of my left eye was a leg kicker, someone with a propeller leg they can't stop moving. People, I am not winning here...picking and kicking. Holy hyperactivity! I decide to look up at the ceiling and then I noticed people around me looking up wondering what I was looking at . . .

So, although I won the bet in my head about the guest suite, it was an unfair win. The building hadn't yet turned on the heat, and it was really cold. Weird mom had my space heater and the oven on when I arrived.

"I knew you wouldn't like it," I said.

She said, "Shelley, I could deal with hair on the toilet and the giant toenail I found in the tub, which by the way I sprayed the shit out of. It's just too COLD!"

She was right. It was too cold, and even though you can't pick and kick your family, I love my mom . . . we all come with baggage.

CHAPTER 64

Skinny jeans

Many of you know there are several things I don't get in life, like vegans, and why people don't say hello in elevators. Well, again, I am totally perplexed about something, and that something is skinny jeans.

I don't understand skinny jeans. I don't understand why people like them, wear them, or buy them. If I want something to hug my calves that tight, I would get a dog that follows me around and humps my legs all day.

I'm all for accepting your body and showing off your figure, but I don't care who you are or what you look like, to me, no one looks good in skinny jeans.

If leggings aren't pants, then why are skinny jeans pants? They essentially fit as tight as leggings. Is it because they have a zipper? Is that the differentiator?

In order to help my confusion, I bought my very own pair of skinny jeans. Being me, I bought an expensive pair of skinny jeans, in fact a pair of purple skinny jeans, hoping the color would hide the fact that I was wearing the very jeans I think no one looks good in.

On a couple occasions, I put on the skinny jeans and promptly took them off. I would almost rather walk around naked because then I could show off my tattoo, which I think looks better on me than skinny jeans.

I don't think people should be sporting mom jeans, and not everyone needs to be wearing boot-cut, but I just don't understand why people love skinny jeans. I wonder if people who like skinny jeans think skinny jeans make them look skinny, as opposed to skinny referring to the cut?

So today, I decided to embrace my purple skinny jeans and try to make friends with them. Why? Because I'm weird...why else? I put them on and decided no matter what or where I had to go today, I would make friends with these jeans, that is until I started writing this story.

Now I have to go change for dinner.

CHAPTER 65

Smell my dog

"Smell my dog!" I announced in the lobby yesterday. My rescue dog Potato had a bath and he smelled so good, people actually stopped to smell my dog and we all liked it.

Any olfactory, I often forget to shave my underarm hair. Either that or I am just rebellious, but most likely I am simply lazy about it. I don't have much underarm hair any way.

Any hairy pit, years ago, my weird mom was very ill and put in a medically-induced coma. My sister, my weird dad and I lived in one hotel room in Baltimore, while my mom was in Hopkins. Notice I did not use the adjective *weird* before the word *sister*. We can just call her *special*.

Apparently, I was suffering from Sleeping Tourette's according to my special sister who informed me I shouted out expletives during the night. Any father issues, one day during this horrific experience, I said to my sister "Hey, let's not shave our underarm hair until Mom gets better."

She said, "Okay."

It was months before my mom got well. We actually were told to make funeral arrangements and say goodbye to her. My weird mom is a truly a weird miracle!

Have you ever walked by someone's apartment and smell dirty clothes? Did I ever tell you that when I was married, we could smell dirty clothes from one guy's apartment? The guy who lived there looked just like Bryan Adams, and every time we walked by, even if we were in the middle of an argument, we would simultaneously growl, "Cuts like a knife."

The only problem was, this guy was no Bryan Adams, he was just a smelly alcoholic air-traffic controller. Holy two out of three words you never want to hear in the same sentence!

Any smell, I think I have a new calling. If you are feeling down, I'll sing to you. Just call me. Yesterday, my friend was down and I thought it might help if I sang, "Hey, hey, what can I do," by Led Zeppelin. Potato doesn't know how to play any instruments, and my pretend band wasn't home, so I sang acapella until she laughed and I laughed.

Love, Shelley

WEIRD GIRL ADVENTURES

CHAPTER 66

Stain

You can call it a yukata, kimono, schmata, housecoat, dressing gown. In my house, we call it "stain." Yes, that's right, *stain*. Remember the scene in *Game of Thrones*?

"A sinner comes before you, Cersei of House Lannister. She has confessed her sins and begged for forgiveness. To demonstrate her repentance, she will cast aside all pride, all artifice, and present herself as the gods made her . . . to you, the good people of this city."

Okay, well, if you didn't watch GOT, a woman basically has to do the walk of shame. Not the mascara-smudged, ripped pantyhose, lost-a-patent-leather-black-pump-1980s-type of WOS. This walk of shame requires the character to repent for her sins by walking naked down the main road while onlookers repeatedly exclaim, "Shame, shame, shame." They also throw poop at her.

Bonus—GOT trivia: The actress who played Cersei was pregnant at the time, so they asked a double to grow a full bush (unless they used a hair piece) to do the WOS.

Any milk of the poppy, in my home, I do the Walk of Stain. It goes something like this:

I walk into the living room wearing my robe, aka stain, no stunt double here, just me whose bush status is none of your beeswax unless you are an aesthetician, and my boyfriend Mark chants, "Stain. Stain. Stain," ad nauseum.

Why? Thanks for asking. I'll tell you why.

> It is literally impossible for me
> to eat or drink anything without
> spilling on my robe.

So wait, I know what you are thinking. You're like, "Shelley be like spilling shit all over her shit like all the time? What happens when she goes out to eat?"

Here's the deal. Somehow by the grace of God, I actually manage to be more adept at utilizing utensils and drinking vessels when in public. *Whoa!* Come to think of it, I am actually better at not spilling in public than Mark.

I love a robe. Do you feel me on this one? Some people don't get this whole robe thing. I just love a robe! In fact, if I were to rate my favorite clothing items, I would have to say next to my ciraca 2007 green dress, a robe is a close second. Now, this could change as the green dress may only have one or two more summers left.

If you don't know the green dress I am referring to, check out every other photo on my Facebook feed during the warmer months for the past twelve years. It has been washed so many times, it's almost like my outdoor robe except I don't usually spill things on it.

This morning I ran into my friend, Bev, who shares my love of robes. When I told her I was going to write this story, she very animatedly told me about her "robes of many colors," and that a robe was like a "clothing hug." Okay, Bev, I am paraphrasing about the colors but not the hug. I totally agree with you.

Whenever my boyfriend Mark doesn't get something I do, or no one in his family or basically no one he has ever known has ever done said thing, he usually categorizes it as, "It must be a Jewish thing."

And because Mark is lifelong non-Jew as well as a non-robe wearer and doesn't get the whole robe thing, and somehow once saw at least one other Jew who wore a robe, maybe in a Woody Allen film, to him, robes are a Jewish thing.

I am not sure where my love of a good robe comes from. My mom always bought us fancy Lanz of Salzburg nightgowns. I loved them as a little girl, however I haven't worn a nightgown in decades. I only wear pajamas, well more accurately some type of tattered bottom and ill-fitting, one-boob-revealing top.

I think my dad had a robe. Some sort of non-Jewish, gentiley, Christmasy, plaid robe. I think I may have borrowed or stolen that robe from him, and the rest is history.

Since the beginning of my robe-wearing journey, I have had some great robes. I mean really great robes! Many a plush hotel robe, some terry, some organic cotton, and I remember one special Christmas gift robe from an ex-boyfriend—that robe outlasted several relationships.

My current light-gray robe was purchased three years ago from Nordstrom, now allegedly affectionately referred to as Stain.

Being an expert robe wearer, I have established a set of robe-wearing commandments that must be followed and, again, are referred to in my home as, "It must be a Jewish thing."

1. Thou shalt wear a robe when eating dinner at home in order to catch any and every spill to retain its status as Stain.

2. Thou shalt not wear a robe at dinner without some type of bottom and top underneath to cover the wayward-boob thing.

3. Thou shalt not wear a robe post a.m. shower due to thy internal body temperature fluctuations that cause sweating.

4. Thou shalt not take out the garbage after dinner without wearing thy robe.

5. Thou shalt put all garbage in thy robe pocket including but not limited to used Q-tips, tissues and wadded up paper towels when thou is more than five feet from a trashcan.

6. Thou shalt put wax earplugs removed from ears when rising in the morning and be certain to forget to remove them before washing thy robe.

So I shall end with a little poem:

ODE TO THE ROBE

There's nothing like a robe when you're
sick with a bug

Like my friend, Bev, says, a robe is "like a
hug."

You may spill, you may drip, and feel
really lame.

You can throw it in the wash and do the
walk of shame.

You can wear it to the store or down the
hall.

You can have different colors for spring
and for fall.

You may have one with a zipper to pull
over your head.

If you're really cold, you can wear it to
bed.

Hugh Hefner wore a robe but the bunnies
did not.

The Big Labowski wore one to carry his
pot.

Rabbi, Priest, Gentile or Jew

Oy, do I have a robe for you!

One day a new robe I shall obtain, but for now I'm quite
happy with...

"Stain, stain, stain, stain, stain," ad nauseum.

CHAPTER 67

Still

I could feel the vibrations coursing through my body. The freight train was coming, and it was coming fast. In a split second, I was on it.

I didn't know where it was going, I only knew it was fast. I wasn't sure what stops it would make or how long it would take to get there. Most of the freight trains I've taken stopped at familiar destinations including Fear, Incessant Worry, Anger, Lash Out, Tears, and I'm Sorry. One line stopped at Stuck, Panic, as well as the intersection of Always and Never.

I could get off at any stop. Often I would get off at every stop and then get right back on.

When the train finally pulled into the end-of-the-line station called Exhaustion, I'd get off, tired and emotionally drained from the ride until I could feel the vibrations of the next train headed my way . . .

I left Chicago the summer of 2010, and moved to North Carolina. I wanted a warmer climate and honestly some geographical separation from my life as I had known it.

I identified myself as an athlete. I was a marathoner and a spin instructor. My desire was to do fifty marathons and spend most of my time running and biking outdoors. While I loved running, my running community and the many lifelong friends I've made as a result, running provided me with an identity. It also provided me an emotional escape from my incessant fear and worry. I had used everything else you can think of to shut off my mind, and all attempts, while effective short-term, were ultimately ill-fated.

By 2012, the identity I thought was mine was stripped away. In fact, my entire life turned upside down. I had suffered a spinal injury and was no longer able to run. In fact, I could hardly walk, lost my job, rehomed my dog, had two more surgeries, and was away from home, I was no longer able to spend time with my running community, and my support consisted of a boyfriend who was becoming a ghost of his former self by slipping into a horrible drug addiction.

I've had anxiety my entire life but this catapulted me into a whole new level. This was trauma—chronic pain syndrome resulting in terror and PTSD.

I began to tremble incessantly, was unable to sleep, and barely able to function. I spent days just sobbing and panicking from the fear of being in so much pain every day, watching my boyfriend disappear from realty, while losing my own. Even when I was no longer staying with him, I was terrified of what was happening to him. When I closed my eyes I would see the thugs, dealers and crackheads that had been around. I didn't know how to get out. I also didn't know who I was or how to live in this world without having an escape from my own fear.

I returned to Chicago in 2013. Through an enormous amount of support from friends from a twelve-step program and some additional help, spiritual and otherwise, I finally got the strength to find some pieces of myself, meds to get some sleep, and financial help to come back home.

I processed a lot of my emotions through writing, a gift for which I am truly thankful. I felt safe back in Chicago. I started expressing myself creatively through photography, art and writing. No longer wearing the false identities I had worn my entire life. As long as I had structure, the anxiety seemed to be kept at bay, but throw a curveball my way and I jumped right back on the train.

No one was exempt from my fear, worry and anger at various levels of escalation.

Work really triggered my anxiety. I wanted so badly to be an energetic badass like I thought I had been before everything took me down, but I panicked and would sabotage myself. The jobs I held over the past few years triggered my anxiety to the point where I was paralyzed. I would lose control emotionally, and it extended into my relationships and friendships where I would just come off helpless and angry, and then feel such guilt and remorse as a result of my reactions.

A friend who has known me for more than half my life pointed out that this was sort of the final frontier in that I was no longer using anything external to deal with my emotions. Although it was better than some of the other things I had done to cope, the bondage of fear and emotional instability were simply not enough.

You're late; I'm going to bite your head off.

The deal hasn't closed; I'm going to worry until it's painful and then just cry.

The job is too stressful. You created an unhealthy environment and it's unfair. Endless what-ifs and no-I-can't-do-that, making my life smaller in order to avoid the unknown.

I didn't know what GAD, generalized anxiety disorder, was. I thought it was some diagnosis for insurance purposes, like, "It's not specifically related to anything, it's just general."

I didn't know I had a classic case, and that those of us with GAD exhibit so many of the same behaviors. No one ever explained it to me.

By saying that I have GAD by no means takes away my responsibility to manage my anxiety, nor is it an excuse for my being the freight train in other people's lives.

I just never knew why I trembled, why my thoughts raced, why I was afraid to do anything out of my comfort zone, why I sabotaged my own success, and why my reactions went from zero to ten so quickly.

I finally saw a doctor who explained that when someone has anxiety, a traumatic event can totally disrupt the wiring of your nervous system and when perceived threats occur, your nervous system doesn't really know the difference between perceived and real. You react in flight, fright or freeze mode as if you were being attacked.

It's not a cognitive reaction. It's a nervous system reaction. I tried so many different ways to change my reaction but was unsuccessful.

Now I understand what GAD is, and what happens as a result. This knowledge has been extremely helpful. More important, I'm now learning ways to manage the anxiety through mindfulness, learning how to respond as opposed to reacting.

This means I can jump the track and miss the train!

Everyone knows fear is a liar, and worry is about the past and the future. People with anxiety get attached to the outcomes they perceive in their head, and those stories become the truth. The idea of "maybe it will, maybe it won't," scares the crap out of people with anxiety.

The combination of mindfulness, meditation and hatha yoga are helping me slow down, be present and in awareness. I'm able to recognize when my body begins to feel stressed. I now have that moment to be present for what's going on and I can look at the thought, take a breath and not attach to it like or lean into it. I now have a choice point.

Choice equals freedom.

Like any practice, I'm not going to do this perfectly, however I am committed to continue the practice of mindfulness and continuously help myself to have a better stress response as opposed to stress reaction.

I hope that anyone who suffers from excessive worry, anxiety or depression will see from this story that there is another way.

Thank you to all my friends in Chicago, North Carolina, and everywhere for walking through this life with me.

CHAPTER 68

Story, by River the dog

Where the heck are the rabbits? What happened? Why are we here? I don't understand.

The other day I got picked up for doggy daycare and then the craziest, messed up thing happened. The doggy daycare lady took me somewhere I had never been. She had to carry me through the front door because the man told her I wasn't allowed to walk. Wait, what? I just don't get it. Why am I not allowed to walk?

So we get in the elevator. I've been in one before but this one takes a lot longer and everything smells different, and I just don't get it. Angie, the daycare lady, knocks on a door and then WTF? There's my mom like nothing happened. I lick her face and run around to smell everything. Some things smell right but other things don't smell right at all. I see some of my toys and Mom gives me some peanut butter.

Mom's friend, Chris, comes over, and I know him because he took care of me when Mom travelled last week. They take me for a walk but there's no grass, just cement. Where am I supposed to go poop? Ahhhh, finally some little speck of grass. I do my business and we go back home.

I'm really confused. Mom seems really busy unpacking and I'm just wandering around. I then realize there is this big window and I can see a bunch of stuff. Mom sees me looking out. She opens the doors and I walk out but there are bars, so I can't walk out too far, only my head. It's weird. I am outside but I'm kind not because I can't get anywhere. Mom lets me back in and I'm so confused I just lay down on the couch. A while later, she joins me and then we go to bed. I know this bed and I am comforted by the way my mom holds me.

The next day we go to a park. I don't know this park. Where are the frickin' rabbits? This is not the park I know. There are all these dogs hanging out with each other and that's all fine and good but I want to find something to kill. What? Wait a minute. My mom is not holding my leash. I run and run and run. I hear here calling me but I don't care.

"River . . ."

"River . . ."

"River . . ."

I don't give a rabbit's ass. She can call all she wants. Give me a duck, anything. She finally catches me and is holding the leash again. We go back to that strange place and I head to my new favorite spot besides the balcony—the closet. It's dark in there and everything smells familiar.

We go for another walk today which was cool. I found a partially eaten bagel with cream cheese. Score, until my mom rips it out of my mouth and throws it too far for me to snatch.

We go into a store with moving stairs. I'm scared. They're moving up and I want to run back down but Mom doesn't let me. We go back outside. OMG! I find all these yummy chicken wing bones but Mom keeps yanking them from my mouth.

So now we are back at this strange place again. Maybe we are going to stay here. Maybe if I go to sleep for a bit and dream about chicken bones, bagels and cream cheese, and rabbits, when I wake up, things will be back to normal.

Love,

River

"Cat-tat-stromi"

CHAPTER 69

Texaco

When I was seven, I thought that when I grew older I would become a fat mumu-clad grandma living in the state of Texaco, in a camper that we, all twenty of us, including my four kids and their kids, had driven to Hawaii along with the Jewish version of my live Ken doll-husband, who would also be fat and grandfatherly. Whether he had genitalia at that time was irrelevant, as was the fact that one can't drive to Hawaii from Texaco, or anywhere else for that matter.

I sat in the backseat of our taupe Oldsmobile Delta 88, obviously without a seatbelt, while both Mom and Dad chain-smoked: his cigarette of choice, filterless Camel; her choice, Parliament.

I am sure my sister was in the car with me, but I don't remember, as I was much too busy living in a bubble of my own fantasy world, later to become these stories.

I don't know how I could see through the billows of stinky smoke but there it was, the big red star with the letter T in the middle. That's it! I want to move to Texaco. It just had to be a really groovy place. This was during the time, one of the few times, I should add, when my sister and I were communicating without physically harming each other, to devise our master plan to save up our allowance to buy a camper and drive to Hawaii.

I guess after tiring of hula lessons and Don Ho concerts in all his *Tiny Bubbles* glory, in my mind, unbeknownst to my sister, I became the Keeper of the Camper, which I would later take to Texaco and apparently keep for the rest of my life to schlep around the twenty members of my non-birth-control-taking wanna-be a Catholic family.

As you may recall, I was obsessed with Barbie and a good camper, especially the one and only Barbie Country Living Camper. Holy Hippiness! This would be the perfect camper to drive to Hawaii and later Texaco!

This bright yellow-and-orange dream vehicle with its resplendent rainbow, birds, and flowers was the grooviest ride ever! It had a sliding door, a stove, and one outdoor chair. Did I say one chair? Yes. Yes, I did. It wasn't until years later that I realized the real reason Skipper was always tagging along.

The closest I ever got to Hawaii during my youth was a childhood favorite. If you are from Chicago, you may remember the Kona Kai. Once in a while we piled in the Delta '88 for a family outing to the Kona Kai restaurant at the O'Hare Marriott. Even my own fantasy-filled imagination could not have created the splendor and magic of this place—dark bamboo, tropical plants, beautiful waitresses, and the best part, drinks in pineapples and Tiki-shaped drinkware with umbrella stirrers and plastic flowers. Holy Teriyaki!

I have never been to Texaco. Have you?

Mahalo!

"Coffee & Donuts".

Why is there a tea kettle? This is a coffee cottage

Service with a smile :)

Endless coffee! Want Some?

Christa, my friend, is obsessed with donuts!

My version of how I would look after transforming from glamour to Ample bosomed grandma.

CHAPTER 70

Thanksgiving

I was afraid. It was Thanksgiving 1981. I was all alone in my dorm room on the tenth floor of the west tower at Ithaca College in upstate New York. I was one of a handful of eight thousand students who hadn't gone home for the holiday, and was too afraid to leave my room.

Holy isolation, I went from cold to cold. The cold wind whistled and whipped up snow, blowing it around in cascades of white sparkles. Frost scaled its way up the windows. I'd look out and see complete stillness, not one human being in sight.

There were several dorms scattered across campus but the cafeteria in my dorm was closed. The only open cafeteria was down at the Student Union, and for some reason I was afraid to go. Maybe it had to do with the movie *The Shining*, which had come out the previous year.

So there I was, alone in a dorm room on Thanksgiving.

I lived on hot air popcorn, room temperature cans of Tab, and Marlboro cigarettes for four days. I would fill up the air popper machine with just the right amount of popcorn kernel, put the so-called directional plastic top on, turn the thing on, plug my ears from its jet propeller noise, and get ready for the thing to explode every which way except for the bowl beneath it. After cleaning up the strays, I'd sprinkle the popped kernels with a little bit of Tab to moisten them enough to make the salt stick. The only sounds I heard during those few days were the crunch of the non-soggy pieces of popcorn and whatever TV station the rabbit ears could pick up.

Subsequent Thanksgiving were sometimes better, sometimes not.

One thing I'm forever reminded of on this particular holiday is how for many years I was glued to the TV in my little flannel, floral Lanz nightgown, sitting way too close as usual in a position that inevitably evoked a sharp tone of admonishment from my mother warning me, "If you keep sitting that way you will become knock kneed," as the magical floats of the Macy's Thanksgiving Day parade went by.

I wasn't interested in the giant Goofy or Santa. I wanted to see the princesses waving like glamorous perfect living Barbies atop floats covered in fake snow and dreamy scenes.

My father would come down the stairs at some point and without fail, every year he would say the following, "We were too poor to go to the parade."

My dad grew up in Bayonne, New Jersey, less than an hour by public transportation to NYC. It wasn't until many years later he realized the reason his family didn't go to the Macy's parade is because they were Jewish. Parades are free.

Life is funny. I no longer eat hot air popcorn and my dad is no longer with us, but parades are still free, and I still have that wistful little girl inside who loves pretty princesses on pretty floats.

I have happy memories of past Thanksgivings as well as sad ones. I ran my first race one Thanksgiving morning years ago, and ran my last race on a Thanksgiving not long ago.

I remember my dad's urgent request to spend his last Thanksgiving with him.

Before leaving North Carolina in 2013, I served at a men's homeless shelter in downtown Raleigh one evening each week. It was more self-serving than serving. I was so lost and so lonely, I felt like I had more in common with the men at the shelter, even though I drove there, and could leave to return home to a nice bed although sleep was completely elusive those days.

I would go because I felt welcome. I would go because some of the folks who ran the kitchen were former addicts who told me the truth about someone I loved and didn't want to leave.

This year I won't be with my family. I am spending the day with a friend.

I think we all long for that perfect wonderful holiday. The truth for me is that every day is Thanksgiving. I don't always do it perfectly and I am not free from complaint, longing and desires, however, I am so grateful I don't have adequate words to express it.

Happy Thanksgiving every day!

CHAPTER 71

The girl draggin' the tattoos

I walked into the crowded coffee shop in all my early nineties glory, thigh-high suede boots, black tights, stone-washed cut-offs (repurposed former full-length jeans), black turtleneck, and distressed leather aviator jacket. I scanned the room looking for the man behind the voice. I knew him only by telephone through work. Cautiously, I walked up to a man sitting alone, nerves pulsating through my body. "Are you Tom?"

He replied, "No, I'm not."

Giggling with embarrassment, I wanted to disappear but just as I was turning to walk away, he said "Yes, I'm Tom."

We laughed and I could barely look at him. He was so attractive and sparks flew! About an hour later, Tom asked me what I felt like doing. My response, "I want to get a tattoo."

His response, "Okay, let's go."

That's how it all began.

I can't remember why I wanted a tattoo. I don't think I knew anyone with tattoos at that time. There were no sleeves, tramp-stamps or even barbwire tats around anyone's upper arm that I knew of. I ended up getting a small rose on the back of my hip as Tom sat there and watched with a smile. I had it strategically placed so my mom would never see it.

Upon completion, we were instructed to purchase Preparation H to keep the area moist and protected, which I did, only to realize later when I got home that I had purchased suppositories. Tom and I didn't stay together, and that tattoo was subsequently covered.

My second tattoo was a cup of coffee. Not the Starbucks type of cup with the sleeve. Ironically, Starbucks recently allowed employees to have visible tattoos but not on their face or neck. Sorry Lil Wayne, as if your future destiny involves Frappuccino making...

This tattoo was a classic diner cup and saucer with steam coming from the top. Why? To paraphrase a classic, if you like it you should have put a tattoo on it. Wuh uh oh uh uh oh oh uh oh uh uh oh...

After going Chock Full O' Nuts, the next tat was a vine going down my spine, to connect me to life like the vine that grows from a tree. There were about three major tattoo shops in a ten-mile radius at the time, and pretty much a choice of three genres, traditional, black and gray, and irezumi (I bet I just taught you a new word). We had Sailor Jerry traditional tats, not like the ink of today. I met a really nice guy while getting that one. Too bad he had just been released from prison and I didn't see the possibility of an LTR.

Baxter came next. I woke up on Labor Day morning still wearing my clothes, having overindulged the night before to dull the pain of putting my little five-year-old Pug to sleep. Brokenhearted, I searched through the yellow pages to find a shop that was open on the holiday. On that grief-stricken morning, I had to have a tattoo of Baxter to be with me forever.

Fast forward, two really bad tats from a so-called artist with whom I had a crush (lesson learned, hot does not equal artist and sleeping with him would have been better short-term decision), Bettie Page down my ribcage during my biker phase because she was a force as the queen of pinups, later to become an Evangelical Christian, to then finally covering my disparate tattooed back with one huge traditional back piece.

Injecting a little trivia here. What do you get a woman who has everything for your fortieth wedding anniversary? If you're my late dad, a Mensa and veterinarian born about a decade too premature to be a hippy, you get her name tattooed on your arm. Good thing her name is Jan.

Here I am now, fifty-two years-old, not quite the younger version of myself and certainly not the same person who would make the same tattoo choices again, yet I have no regrets. I now understand why I got them. I was swept away by life to be who I thought I was supposed to be. I didn't yet know how to express myself artistically, so I put art on my body. If I could have them removed, would I? No, they are part of my journey in this weird life. I will always appreciate the art of ink, my art and yours (well, some of yours). I consider myself somewhat of a pioneer, a trailblazer who will pave the way for aging gracefully with ink. In the meantime, I can cover my art in my soul-sucking corporate career yet I can never cover the artist I was born to be.

I thought for a moment, if I were to get any more tattoos, they would be the words *Hope* and *Love*, but I don't need those words in ink. I just need to live by them every day while I am the girl draggin' the tattoos.

Live the journey, learn the lessons, regret not.

CHAPTER 72

The guy who stole Christmas

'Twas the week before Christmas when I picked up the phone to call him. His voice sounded strange and then all of sudden, "Who are you? He's over here wasted and I want to know who you are. John and I have been together for ten months. Who are you?"

I hung up.

Turns out he's a great catch as long as you have really low standards and no sense of self-worth.

Darn it! I wanted Christmas! I bought him a gift. I bought his daughter, sister, and niece a small gift. I wanted spiral ham (not to eat, just to look at). I wanted a big old gentile spread and maybe a little bit of old fashioned, tableside family argument right in the middle of dinner.

I wanted to hear something like "Oh, that's just Uncle Bob, he always drinks too much. He'll stop cursing once we stop laughing."

I would say I wanted to see red cardigans and plaid clothing items but I think only Catholics do that.

Instead I got lied to, the flu, and no Christmas.

You tell me "Go volunteer," and I tell you, "I already do." You can tell me that "It's never that fun with my family," or "You are so lucky you don't have to deal with this," or "It's so stressful."

And I am here to tell you that being raised Jewish, I have, CCE—Cultural Christmas Envy. I want Christmas.

I was fortunate enough to have a few Christmases when I was married. We went all out with a Griswald-like vengeance in our apartment and would spend Christmas day with my ex-husband's family. Complete with his mom-in-law hitting a deer on the way over one year. Isn't that a song? Oh, yeah, Grandma, reindeer... never mind.

Any Ho Ho Hot Mess, it's not just about Christmas. I liked someone who ended up being a liar with a bit of a, shall we say, unhealthy relationship with alcohol, and I guess I'm grateful I found out sooner rather than later. We had been dating for about a month, we were having fun and we did interesting things together, like seeing the new contemporary collection at the Art Institute and a wine-pairing dinner with some of his family members. I never saw him overindulge.

I returned the gifts I had bought his family, and bought myself a new bathrobe. I finally threw out the one I had been wearing for twenty-three years, given to me on Christmas many years ago from a non-liar, non-unhealthy relationship with alcohol ex-boyfriend.

Next year I am having a Griswald-like Christmas party complete with spiral ham to look at or to eat, for anyone who has no place to go. Merry Christmas.

"Queen of Ham"

Always the Queen of the Living Room

I don't eat ham but I am one

Trespian

life is supposed to be like TV right?

It's ok! I'm HERE!
Applause ☺

CHAPTER 73

The contest

The top three contestants were standing in front of their stations waiting for the judge to come inform them of their final challenge.

The judge walks in, "Today, for the finale, you three will draw knives to choose the main ingredient for your meal."

Contestant one swiftly draws a knife from the knife block. The judge says, "You've picked anxiety."

"Okay, next up," she says and brings the knife block over to the next contestant. He pulled out the knife that has "resentment" written on it.

The last contestant draws the remaining knife. "Great. You get impatience. Okay, you finalists have only seconds to run into the pantry of your mind and grab any additional ingredients for your meal."

The three contestants scurry to gather additional ingredients. The judge walks around to see what each contestant is preparing. The judge walks up to contestant number one and asks, "How's it going? What are you making?"

Contestant one replies, "I'm making a mixed grill with my main ingredient, anxiety. I decided to spice it up with a sprinkling of panic and some thin slices of reactivity as well as a jumping to conclusions demi-glace."

Judge, "Okay, sounds great."

Contestant one, too busy in her own head, "What?"

Judge, "I said, it sounds great."

Contestant one wonders if she really means it.

Contestant two is busy working with his main ingredient, resentment, and seems really bothered when the judge comes his way.

"Hi there, what are you making?" the judge asks politely.

"As if you don't already know, I am making a thick stew with coarsely chopped dissatisfaction, bits of bitterness, and I used animosity to thicken the sauce."

Judge, "Alrighty then. I had no idea."

"Alright, everyone. Just a few seconds left," she says while walking over to the contestant number three.

"How are you doing?" the judge asks.

"I'm just trying to finish over here. I messed something up and had to start over, so I've thrown a sandwich together. I made some irritation bread, with thin slices of life's unfair along with delicate and subtle layers of tune you out. I decided to put some interruptions on the side."

"Okay, everyone. Times up. I am going to take some time to think about your dishes and will be back shortly."

After some time, the judge returns. "We have an interesting turn of events. I've had some time to think. The dishes you have prepared will all be thrown out. You'll need to start all over."

"Contestant number one, I offer you peace. Will you accept it?"

"Contestant number two, I offer you acceptance. Will you take it?"

"Contestant number three, I want you to have forgiveness. Is your heart open?

"Congratulations, everyone. You have all won. You are all human, and you are only as good as your last meal."

Turns out the judge was named Self.

" Tech Overload "

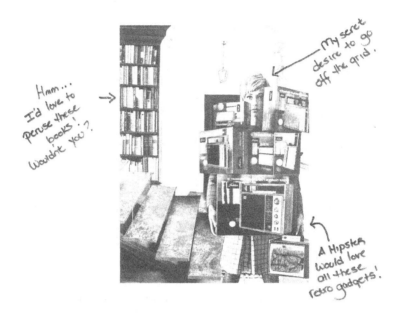

CHAPTER 74

Vaginaing

I felt so squirmy, like I had to tinkle. The discomfort veiling the room was palpable. We sat in our own wiggly weirdness and awe, none of us really daring to look around. We were shadows with tiny occasional giggles escaping from various directions in the room like a Whac-a-Mole game, softly illuminated by the light rays directed at the screen from the filmstrip projector, teacher placed appropriately in the back corner of the room with a site line of a hawk ready and able to shush any uninvited anything from any of us.

"There's a special opening just in front of the place where you have your BM."

Giggle.

"It's very, very tiny for a little girl but as you grow it grows along with you."

Squirm.

"Mature," pronounced "*Ma Tour.*"

Oh God, I really have to pee.

"VAGINA."

"VAGINA."

"VAGINA."

Vagina, how many times would they use that word and, *and* the word penis?"

Oh, my God! We were hearing these words in a classroom. It was all so mysterious, exciting, and so very *clinical.*

This was the start to my very own vaginaing. It's a noun and a journey. An action-filled adventure including humor, drama of . . .

   . . . a peach

   . . . a pussy

   . . . a womb

   . . . and a return home to the filmstrip reflection of the vulva kind, an homage and sort of the everything old is old again reflection of the clinical nature of our sexuality.

Now, I'd like to request your full attention before I go on with this story. There are several emergency exists. Please take a few moments to locate your nearest exit. For some, the nearest exit may be the last paragraph you just read. By all means, please locate the lavatory and use when needed.

Holy fallopian tubes squeeze your Kegels and go with the flow . . . I have no idea where this is taking me, just as I had no idea where my own vaginaing would lead.

I wonder, if fat accumulates around the abdomen, how does it manage to stop at the labia? Hmmm, I have some googling to do. It's not like I haven't googled images of aging vaginas to see if there are any others out there like mine.

Oh, come on, you have, too. Haven't you?

I guess before the internet, people were left wondering. I wish we wondered more. How often have you thought some famous person was dead and suddenly someone makes a reference to them, and you find yourself searching the internet to check to see if they are, in fact, dead?

I wish I still just wondered about many things, including my vagina. Maybe we just knew we couldn't know things and just let it go, because asking one other person wouldn't really give you an aggregated response, just their own version on the truth. But here's the thing, why is it that now we can find out so many things yet no one tells us still, just as they never really did? Things I didn't know until I knew them, like the fact that sex involves motion, it's not just one person laying on top of another. I discovered this after Suave strawberry shampoo was shot up my nostrils during what became an extraordinarily painful game of guess-the-scent by my so-called best friend whose brother would walk me home, trip me, and hump me, hence the motion knowledge.

Finding my parents' copy of the *Joy of Sex* provided me with a cursory understanding that there was something called an orgasm which females could have, too.

My mother told me that if I had sex before marriage, I would go crazy, or something like, "It will psychologically fuck you up." Well, I did go crazy and I was psychologically fucked up, but I don't think that was why.

Those are just a few examples.

Joan Rivers made reference to her aging vagina all the time, yet I really just thought it was because she wasn't sexually active anymore. Did you?

Oh . . . the things you don't know until you know them.

Let me speed things up a bit here. So we go from the film-strip version of our sex organs to the actual *Ma Touring* of our sex organs. For me it was an obsession with getting my period, clueless that within just a few years I'd be sleeping in some sort of landmine trap of six super-sized maxi pads arranged like Jenga blocks following several days of dark red rage and despair. On the flipside, I often enlisted the male variety to utter empathetic painful groans and long elaborated "Owe," moans along with me.

From there we go to the exploration phase of vaginaing which for me was with the most popular boy in school who secretly came over to be with very unpopular, highly bullied me for the purpose of coaching me through all the bases for a few years until we actually completed the grand slam. Funny thing is that despite the fact he kept me a secret, there must have been something very compelling about weird me or my vagina, because we actually still keep in touch to this day.

This next phase of vaginaing is brought to you by daddy issues, the gift that keeps on devaluing your self-worth and essentially devaluing the worth of all women into physical objects. Daddy issues come in packs of years, decades, and even lifetime supplies, all for a very high price. Get yours today and we'll throw in the eating disorder of your choice. I could have said objectifying, but it simply didn't do justice to the commercial break effect. Daddy issues took vaginaing to an entirely new level, a low level fraught with abuse, promiscuity and the proverbial and insidious shame invisibly tattooed on my everything.

Love and marriage, love and marriage go together like a big miscarriage. As I was headed toward the exit door after a last ditch Can This Marriage Be Saved trip to Florida, that included a very unpleasant and unwanted entry resulting in the unexpectedness of expecting until the walls caved into a loss only vaguely remembered with a wistful, how old would he or she be now every so often.

"You'll feel so much better," she said. I'd like to say she said more than that, but that was it, that was all she said.

The cold like I had never felt before following the procedure left me wondering if his penis could sense the void that paled in comparison to the cavernous space waiting to be filled by grief and emptiness.

And then the filmstrip begins again...

Vagina.

Vagina.

Vagina.

And, it's all so very clinical.

Until someone appeared who happens to think my vagina is . . .

. . . a peach

. . . a pussy

. . . a thing of beauty

Even if I think it's all so very clinical.

With or without children, a uterus, a period, or even sex, as long as we are alive, we still have one and, by default, I am still a woman. So are you.

Love,

Shelley

CHAPTER 75

Where there's a shoulder there's always a pad

I typically write short essays or *vignettes,* a noun meaning a brief evocative description, account, or episode. I write vignettes due to the fact that technology is increasingly decreasing our attention spans.

By the way, if this is a new word for you, it's pronounced *vin,* which rhymes with *sin,* which I'll leave to your imagination, and *ette,* which is pronounced like the word *yet* as in, how is it that we don't yet know what this *vignette* is about?

Although this is a vignette, it is not brief due to anyone's attention span; it is due to memory loss, so there just isn't a lot to say. The memory loss isn't due to age, and I will get to that in a moment.

In honor of the '80s coming back in style, I thought I'd write about some of my memories. Although a decade is a long time and a vignette, as you already knew or now know, is a brief account, a vignette will have the capacity to provide you with a comprehensive snapshot of what my life was like during that decade. It will encompass most, if not all, of the memories I have from that period of time. I'd like to blame age but, any alcohol consumption, I was in my twenties.

Mom shrilling, "You have to do more with your life than be a FUCKING COCKTAIL WAITRESS!"

Me yelling and crying, "What do you want me to do?"

Mom still shrilling, "Anything except being a FUCKING COCKTAIL WAITRESS!"

Me in default mode, "I want a LOBOTOMY! I want a LOBOTOMY!"

Mom softening, "You can't have a lobotomy," and then escalating, "You can't be a FUCKING COCKTAIL WAITRESS FOREVER!"

She leaves my room. I pull on my pantyhose, go to the closet and look at my prized Prince poster from his *Controversy* album. Even though I don't care what it sounds like when doves cry, I care that he's shirtless with gold chains and looking quite resplendent in his tiny black briefs. I put on my tuxedo halter top, tie my REAL bowtie, go and get my skirt out of the dryer, throw on my black pumps, walk out the door, and light up a Marlboro Red. I walk through the courtyard, click clack, click clack, as the Latin and Parker kids laugh and play with the joy and abandonment of trust-fund kids.

A block later, click clack, puff puff, I feel something lightly hitting the back of my thighs. Oh, great! I tug on the pantyhose hanging from the top of my skirt's waistband. Shit! Static fucking cling. Hey, it could happen even if I wasn't a FUCKING COCKTAIL WAITRESS.

Any everyone wore pantyhose, just another day being angst-filled me. You're welcome to say my college degree did not help me sell more 2-for-1 drink specials, and I probably wouldn't disagree with you. Puff puff, click clack . . . I want a lobotomy.

Mom shouting from upstairs, "Are you looking for a job? You can't be a FUCKING COCKTAIL WAITRESS with a college degreeeeeeeeee . . ."

I don't answer, pretending to already have had that lobotomy.

I'm in the bathroom smoking and spraying the crap out of my bangs to make them stand tall with a slight curl angling back from my forehead.

Thanks to the miracle that is, was, Aqua Net, I appear about an inch taller. Just above my ears, near my temples, I pull the hair back and place a bobby pin to hold the hair in position. Shhhhhhhhhh, shhhhhhhhhh, shhhhhhh. I plaster it down and immobilize it until said hairspray performs its lacquer, or, shall I say, cement miracle. I remove the bobby pins. Ready to go.

Crap. I can find only one shoulder pad. I scour my '70s childhood pink-trimmed drawers for the de rigueur fashion item. Fuck it, I'll just cut a pair out of some other garment.

I shove the shoulder pads under my t-shirt and throw on my peach jumpsuit, slouchy socks, gold hoop earrings, and my custom-made Moosehead for President jeans jacket. Out the door, down the courtyard, puff puff. "Fuck you, you little trust fund kids."

I am sipping on my Moosehead, chewing gum, smoking a Marlboro while playing drums with Bonnie. Garage band? Nope, just me on my usual stool at the end of the bar using straws or sometimes red licorice sticks to beat on the upside-down faux-wood pretzel bowl. I'm totally annihilating Sheila E's "The Glamorous Life."

Any big thoughts, big dreams . . . oops, drop everything. Time to throw down the straws, licorice, beer, and cigarette.

"Moving forward using all my breath."

Without failure it's just Bonnie and me on the dance floor doing our best "Dancing in The Dark" moves. This particular dance move is all-purpose. You just have to slow it down a bit for "Tainted Love" and speed it up a bit for "Whip it." We use the entire length of our arms to make the widest moves and waste the most amount of space of any dance move ever and since. It's easy to dance, no matter how many beverages.

Holy high impact, I have to finish my cigarette and hurry so I can be in the front row of aerobics with Pepper. Pepper has like a total cult following.

"Step Touch! Step Touch!" Holy grapevine, I am out of breath, sweaty, and need a cig. I start thinking about the health club bar. I mean like, where else can you smoke in the club before I've got to go to the tanning bed?

These people are here again for happy hour. They request my station. I serve them a couple rounds of 2-for-1 drinks. They offer me a shot. I never turn one down. Next thing you know, I am no longer a FUCKING COCKTAIL WAITRESS.

I am now standing in the lobby of the Westin Michigan Avenue wearing a uniform, pantyhose, and the four-color Dior eyeshadow palette like my lids are wishing everyone happy 4th of July.

"Welcome to the Westin Michigan Avenue. Are you looking for Katz Bar Mitzvah?"

If I wasn't a lobby greeter, I would be filing keys with my FUCKING COLLEGE DEGREEEEEEEEEE.

Viva la vignette!

ACKNOWLEDGMENTS

First I'd like to thank Led Zeppilin, the Rolling Stones and the Black Crowes. No, not because it sounds cool and not because the lead singer of each group has been my pretend boyfriend at one time or another. It's because during that crazy summer of 2020, yes, that one, the pandemic one where the only life I had was the online kind, and I got so overwhelmed by the social overload I just stopped and started listening to the music of the previously mentioned groups. When I did, the endless creative possibilities dancing in my mind started coming out through collage, art, writing and the decision to take these weird stories from my weird life and put them in a book. So yes, thank you Robert, Mick and Chris (I know they'll be really excited I remembered them in my acknowledgements).

Any magical thinking and rockstar drinking, the real rockstar to whom I will forever be a groupie is Mark Brown, who endured the pre-mindfulness version of me, a very unflattering version for which Mark, while slayed by my middle-age hotness, must have known there was more than meets the eye-candy! I thank him for his love, support, patience, hand-holding (literal, touch is his love language), tucking me in at night and knowing where to put all three pillows, and loving River who came with this epic package.

Endless love and thanks to my mom, the one and only Jan Brown, the self-proclaimed Momma Moth for giving birth to me and waiting for about a half-century for this butterfly to come out of her dark cocoon, for your fierce tenacity and for showing me God is not the only woman who can move mountains.

My sister Lorie, a wonderful woman who never hung up the phone when I went ballistic as she so patiently tried to get me to see I wasn't stuck even though at the time I wasn't able to choose the specific item the universe had to offer me. Although she took the money for the camper we were going to drive to Hawaii, she supported me and paid me back about 1000 times more than the amount we could muster as eight and ten year-olds. Thank you for giving me and the world my nephews, Evan and Jordan, and my niece Jillian.

To my publisher, Lynda Cheldelin Fell of AlyBlue Media. I am crying as I type this and can't find adequate words to thank you for literally standing alongside me as sister, friend, mentor and guide who received my words from the start as if I simply took them from my heart and placed them into yours. And then, AND then, you stood alongside me as if we were chiseling and molding this wonderfully, weird sculpture to showcase to the world otherwise known as this book.

Thank you to my friend and fellow weird girl Kimberly Davis for showing up in life the way you do, for inviting everyone to their own BRAVE, and for penning the foreword to this book, all while moving to a new country. Your deliciously crafted words cover me with the most beautiful sense of what we all long for in life—to be seen, recognized, and known. I feel both humbled and proud. Thank you for embracing me and Shelleyland. I had no idea that my girl crush and love at first Zoom would lead to this.

Thank you to my weird and wonderful friends. some of whom began following along with all the Weird Girl antics born on Facebook followed by LinkedIn and by the wonderful, Dennis Pitocco who allowed me to use my own weirdness of BizCatalyst360. I am deliciously covered by the outpouring of all your abundant love encouragement and weirdness over the years—Judy Anderrson, Jessica Avant, Tera Baker, Kat Barker, Alessandro Bassi, Jason Barnaby, Robin (my Bobin) Bennett,

Caroline Bishop, Bradly Bobich, Emily Black, Anna Blount, Kari Bogdan, Gigi Boynton, Zelda Brafman, Lesa Bricker-Reich, Stephanie Brisson, Tracey Bublick, Pam Bullock, Nancy Joyce Callahan, Carol Campos, Penny Cato, Terri Cenar, Matthew Charles, Catherine Chzanowski, Robert Cutler, Kay Kimbrell Davis, Isabelle Dejols, Tom Dietzler, Jennifer Douglas, Sheila Elizabeth, Jo Dimartino Elsmore, Christa Engel, Lisa Engelberg, Adriana Fieberg, Vicki Flaherty, Beth Steinsmith Fried, Alissa Friedman, Kelly Lemly Garris, Susan Gregory, Alycia Grenesko, Kimberly Hambrick, Melissa Hughes, Jeff Ikler, Kevin Iwomoto, Brooke Jaye, Harriette Katz, Rebecca Keen, Linda Liss, Helen Kane, Caryn Kowswoski, Ilyse Kraft, Michelle Madden, John Maurer, Scott Mason, Bev, McGee, Jennifer McGinley, Laura Mikolaitis, Alicia Miller, Maud Monson, JJ Murray, Don Neske, Lisa Otto, Erica Pear, Kelly Czerniak Pearson, Kelly Port, Jennifer Radler, Aileen Robinson, Andrea Sanchez, Laura Staley, Aaron Skogan, Laurel Swarthout Segal, Andy Vargo, Samy Verdekal.

To those who literally peeled me off the floor when I thought I would never get up—Cheryl Brayton, Deana Vasquez, Margaret Barletta, Wendi Richmond Brown (BFF 4-EVER) and Lauren Raff, Karyn Romer and Marilyn Schanze.

To the wonderful men I love who love me back and not just for my "all thatness," Tom Blondell, Tom Jacob, Met Delipi, Tom Maisel, KJ, Ben Friedman, Mitchel Stern.

My crossover friends from LinkedIn into real life, thanks to the amazing Sarah Elkins and Mike Vicanti, Brian Kelly, Oleg Lougheed and Dennis Pitocco, (double mention much deserved) I love you and thank you for being in my life and for connecting me with countless wonderful people through NLV, Overcoming Odds, HumansFirst and BizCatalyst360.

Although I felt like a total misfit throughout the majority of my career, the love I received from Linda McNairy, Dan Marks, Nina Ramos, Louis Ford and Abby Hart helped me see worth in myself. I deeply appreciate and will never forget it.

Some recent relationships I want to thank for inspiring me include Teresa Quinlin and Ryhs Thomas, who envisioned this book before I did.

To Zach Messler for being you, helping me in the countless ways only you could, and for inviting me to consider that I am a speaker which led to meeting the incomparable Tricia Brouk, Angeliqu Santana, Keiya Rayne, Gayle Damiano, Kristen Donnelly, Jazz Biancci, Kate Mackinnon and Maria Johnson and the Big Talk Community! Cheers to my future TED talk!

It's imperative for me to thank Dr. Christopher Chroniak of the Insight Center—Chicago, who invited me to understand that I wasn't broken for the first time in life, and for leading the lifechanging Mindfulness Based Stress Reduction course that began the great reset of my wiring to my default state of joy.

Dr. Craig Johnson, thank you for being a lifeline for me and a pioneer in the field of eating disorders treatment, for your tireless research to seek new treatment modalities and educate in service of the millions of people who suffer from these insidious disorders.

To my sock monkey, Monk Monk, for bearing witness without judgement to almost 99% of everything that occurred in this weird book, well everything that took place in the last forty-seven years that is.

To you, dear weird readers! Thank you so much for reading OUR book. My weirdness honors your weirdness.

Love,

Shelley

ABOUT SHELLEY BROWN

A corporate strategist who spent 25 years practicing the fine arts of mergers, acquisitions, downsizings, public-private transitions, acts of God, performance reviews, KPIs, workplace cultures, and so much more, Shelley kept  her weird to herself . . . until as an ultra-runner, her vertebrae collapsed, forcing her to rethink who she was and why.

Through this adversity, Shelley learned to allow her individuality to shine through, tapping into her extreme creativity and fearlessness to make a greater impact on the world. This confidence—along with a lifetime serving the hospitality, technology, and convention markets—gave Shelley the unique opportunity to make a remarkable difference, building a program that helped countless leaders and employees learn to be the drivers of their own awareness so they could become more effective, productive, and present.

A bold speaker, future NY Times best-selling author, and incredible ball of positive energy, Shelley has learned to allow her W.E.I.R.D to shine through, turning it from a label to a way of being. Her pandemic resume includes writing a book, launching a greeting card line, and becoming a self-taught pop artist.

Incredibly engaging and fun, Shelley encourages audiences to allow their W.E.I.R.D., embracing individuality to land at a place of inclusion.

Email: shelley@weirdgirladventures.com
Website: www.WeirdGirlAdventures.com
Facebook: Facebook.com/weirdgirladventures
Instagram: Instagram.com/weirdgirladventures
Clubhouse: Shelley Brown @weirdgirl

ARTIST STATEMENT

Growing up as an odd, chubby, artsy child in the early 1970s, I aspired to become Barbie, a stewardess or a Playboy Bunny. With my untreated addiction to candy, paper dolls, Vogue and House Beautiful magazines as well as Colorforms, I lived for anything to take me away into a fantasy world of pointy breasted, high-fashion, feminine whimsy. Later in life, after my nineteenth nervous breakdown in the corporate world, I returned to my artistic roots reflecting my childhood passions.

My collages are quirky little left-of-center stories; each appears to be one cohesive image but upon closer inspection, like a little drop down the rabbit hole, the collective components find their way together to create a delicious, maybe even a little disorienting, marriage of vintage and modern composition. I never know what I am going to create. I start in search of a muse and then build from there.

My mission is to delight. Just like life, with collage, anything can happen. Mostly, the collection is grounded in joy. My hope is that it brings some to you.

Love,

Shelley

PUBLISHED BY ALYBLUE MEDIA
Real stories. Real people. Real inspiration.
www.AlyBlueMedia.com

CPSIA information can be obtained
at www.ICGtesting.com
Printed in the USA
BVHW041148210621
610129BV00014B/229